IMPERATIVES IN EDUCATION

Published by:
American Association of School Administrators
1201 Sixteenth Street, Northwest
Washington, D.C. 20036

Library of Congress Catalog Card Number: 66-18448

Single copy, $6
2-9 copies, 10 percent discount
10 or more copies, 20 percent discount

FOREWORD

In the spring of 1964 AASA President J. Win Payne appointed a special commission and charged it with responsibility for identifying and stating in clear and concise fashion major educational imperatives that must be at the forefront as curriculums are modified, instructional methods revised, and organizational patterns reshaped to meet the educational needs of this country in one of its most dynamic periods.

The members of this commission have had many years of experience as teachers, superintendents, and university faculty members; they have over the past many years regularly met with school boards, with committees of lay citizens, and with faculty members to initiate and develop plans and procedures for dealing with crucial educational problems; and they are sensitive to the needs of children, to the pressures of society, and to the hard facts of budgetary appropriations.

After two years of study, this commission has identified the following nine *imperatives in education:*

To make urban life rewarding and satisfying

To prepare people for the world of work

To discover and nurture creative talent

To strengthen the moral fabric of society

To deal constructively with psychological tensions

To keep democracy working

To make intelligent use of natural resources

To make the best use of leisure time

To work with other peoples of the world for human betterment.

The imperatives identified in this publication are not intended to be educational goals, nor do they encompass the entire educational program. Rather, they are points at which the educational program must be revised and reshaped to meet the needs of the times. To the extent that they are useful to school administrators and other educational leaders in meeting and dealing with crucial educational problems they will have served their purpose.

Forrest E. Conner
Executive Secretary

ACKNOWLEDGMENTS

This publication is the result of team effort. Close working relationships among all members of the Commission were maintained from the earliest planning stage until the volume was completed. No majority or minority points of view are expressed; it is in every respect a commission report. Throughout its two years of work, the Commission drew unsparingly on the experiences of teachers and administrators in many school systems and gratefully acknowledges the valuable assistance of demographers, sociologists, curriculum specialists, and psychologists who graciously granted permission to use information from their publications.

The Commission is indebted to George B. Brain and Forrest E. Conner for their encouragement and support throughout its work. Special acknowledgment is made to Beatrix Sebastian who worked with the Commission from beginning to end in the preparation of manuscripts and editing, to William J. Ellena who prepared the index, to Jane Power for final editing, and to John D. Voss for layout.

AASA Commission on Imperatives in Education

SHIRLEY COOPER, *Chairman*
Director of Inservice Education
American Association of
School Administrators
Washington, D.C.

JOHN S. CARTWRIGHT
Professor of Education
Lehigh University
Bethlehem, Pennsylvania

GEORGE H. DEER, Dean
The Junior Division
Louisiana State University
Baton Rouge, Louisiana

HERBERT W. SCHOOLING, Dean
College of Education
University of Missouri
Columbia, Missouri

CLARENCE SENIOR, Member
Board of Education of the
City of New York
Brooklyn, New York

HOWARD C. SEYMOUR, Superintendent
Union High School System
Phoenix, Arizona

ALLEN H. WETTER
Retired Superintendent of Schools
Philadelphia, Pennsylvania

Special contributor to the report:

GORDON I. SWANSON
Professor of Education
University of Minnesota
Minneapolis, Minnesota

CONTENTS

IMPERATIVE

1 · IMPERATIVES IN EDUCATION

Any thoughtful person who scans in broad perspective and with deep discernment the total educational program in this country cannot escape seeing the relationship of the school to the life of people in cities, towns, and open country places. What the school is and what it has done since the beginning of public education in this country have been inextricably related to the wants and needs of people—to their hopes and expectations, to the ideals that give direction to their thoughts and actions, and to the circumstances in which they live. The values which people cherish; the priorities assigned to these values; the theories that hold promise for giving a sense of order, unity, and efficiency to what people do; and the cultural climate that prevails at any given time in large measure shape the educational program.

By their very nature the schools are oriented toward the future. For the most part they serve young people—young people who look forward to rich, productive, satisfying lives. This is America's promise to its youth. These young people, whether they live in cities, small towns, or country villages or in the wide stretches of the open country, look forward to the time when they will have jobs, homes, families, places in community life that give them opportunity to serve their fellowmen in some useful way, and recognition as individuals with true worth and dignity—a time when they will be mature citizens in a country of which they can be justly proud.

There are at midpoint in the decade of the sixties more than 42 million children and youths enrolled in the public elementary and secondary schools of this country and approximately 5 million more enrolled in private and parochial schools. If present trends and conditions continue to prevail, about one third of these young people will go to college after completion of the secondary grades, another third will end their formally organized education with graduation from high school, and the remaining third will drop out of high school before graduation with less than adequate preparation for effective participation in the world about them.

The public schools are committed to serving all these young people—the gifted, the average, and the less academically talented. All are important; each has an inalienable right to do the best he is capable of doing; and to the extent that anyone fails to develop his full potential and to use it for worthy purposes the country is weaker and democracy has fallen short of achieving its high purpose. To design and support an educational program that will serve them all—not in the same way, but in ways adapted to their different capabilities and needs—is a challenge to all people who have responsibility for planning, supporting, and operating an educational program. The strength and future well-being of the country depend in large measure upon the manner in which people in every local school district, in every county, in every state, and in the nation as a whole respond to this challenge.

The schools serve not only individuals as such, but the totality of society as well—society with its ideals, its values, its purposes, its commitments, its institutions, its enterprises, its governmental processes. These two ends are in no way contradictory. They are but two dimensions of the same purpose. In serving the individual, the schools serve society as a whole, for society is but the totality of individual lives, purposes, and actions.

When one looks to the circumstances in which the youth of this generation are maturing, getting an education or failing in the attempt, seeking employment, and striving to carve out places for themselves in the world about them, he sees—

> Technological advance that has created new relationships between people, education, and work, with technical skills and knowledge, mental alertness, and creative capacities taking priority over capacities to endure hard physical labor.

> The specter of unemployment worrying families, frustrating neighborhoods, and haunting political leaders—even at a time

when there are more people employed in this country than ever before.

More young people entering the labor force when job opportunities in the unskilled and simpler occupational fields are markedly decreasing.

Science and mathematics becoming increasingly important in almost every facet of the total culture and affecting the lives of people in every family and neighborhood in a vital way.

The security of the nation as a whole dependent upon the expansion of economic enterprise and upon scientific advancement.

Consuming ideological conflict gripping the world, with much of the public budget, much public policy, much effort in military defense, much of the economic resources of the country, and much of the thoughts of people devoted to meeting this challenge.

Common problems and issues submitted to the people for decision at the ballot box becoming increasingly complex and of greater consequence.

Rapid advance in communication and travel bringing nations all over the world into closer touch with one another and increasing the need for better understanding of the cultures, institutions, mores, languages, and goals of all peoples.

Mass migration of people from the open country and smaller towns and villages to large centers of population and from the centers of cities to the suburbs, with the inevitable consequences of cultural clashes that shake institutions, disturb long-established customs, set values in new perspective, color political action, disrupt systems of school support, and leave indelible marks on the behavior patterns and characters of children.

Different ethnic, racial, and cultural groups of people vigorously struggling for recognition, full rights, fair employment practices, nondiscrimination in housing, and higher levels of living.

Pressure tactics, emotional displays, and florid propaganda displacing reason and the exercise of sober judgment in approaches to the solution of common problems.

Demands for education beyond the high school exceeding the capacities of institutions of higher learning, with rising standards for admission and escalating tuition charges.

These cultural circumstances are alive with challenges to the schools. The powerful forces that generate cultural change and lead to these circumstances have true meaning only as they affect the lives of individuals—family groups, clusters of people, whole communities, and the institutions that serve them. Without innovations, new approaches, and new emphases in the educational program, the schools will fall short of achieving the high purposes they are expected to achieve.

IMPERATIVE

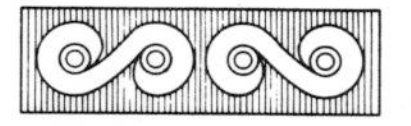

2 · TO MAKE URBAN LIFE REWARDING AND SATISFYING

Education from kindergarten through graduate school throbs with pressures of population growth, population mobility, and cultural change. Public school enrollment has grown in the course of a single decade from 29.9 million to 42.8 million, an increase of about 43.1 percent. The instructional staff has increased by 55.4 percent; expenditures for current expense purposes have increased 153.1 percent, from $7.3 billion in 1954-55 to $18.6 billion in 1964-65; and annual expenditures for capital outlay purposes have increased 30.5 percent, from $2.5 billion to $3.2 billion.[1] Population mobility and social change with broad implications for education have added to the difficulty of school support and administration.

A sustained trend toward urbanization has reduced the school population in sparsely settled rural areas, necessitating further school district reorganization; increased enrollments in suburban school districts; and substantially changed the character of the total population and the school enrollment in the hearts of great cities. People in great numbers have come to the large cities seeking better jobs, better education for their children, and a better way of life. They have come on the crest of a wave of rising human aspirations that is worldwide.

Rural people migrating to the cities bring with them unique educational needs. They need help in developing new occupational skills,

[1] National Education Association, Research Division. *Estimates of School Statistics, 1964-65*. Research Report 1964-R17. Washington, D.C.: the Association, 1964.

in getting jobs, in getting acquainted with new neighbors, and in making new friends. The children in these families tend to be overage for their grade placement. Their reading abilities are low. Their vocabularies are limited. Their home conditions are unstable because of difficulties their families are having in getting settled in a new locality. Tensions, inevitably generated as these newcomers try to find a place for themselves in a new community, are transmitted to young children and older youth. At times these tensions are manifested in gang conflicts, truancy, juvenile delinquency, and antagonism toward the schools.

Social problems arising from this process of assimilation that do not have direct relevance to instruction become pressing issues. School boards in large city school systems find it necessary to spend a great deal of their time and effort in dealing with problems emerging from—

Segregated housing

Unemployment

Retraining older workers whose occupations have been disrupted by technological change

Compliance with civil rights laws

The growing power and militance of voluntary organizations and pressure groups

Changing symbols of social status

Greater public acceptance of responsibility for mentally, physically, economically, and socially handicapped people.

The schools have become a stage upon which ills that trouble groups of people are called to public attention. To an increasing extent, broad social issues and questions that do not immediately manifest themselves as educational problems come to the school for consideration and action because the school is the most visible institution of community life. It is not by accident that the school has become a focal point of action in resolving civil rights issues, combating poverty, lessening the unemployment problem, and easing social tensions. The agenda at nearly every large city school board meeting contains items that relate to population growth and mobility—procurement of school building sites, redefining the boundaries of attendance areas, constructing new school plants, employing additional teachers, adding new features to the instructional program, and securing additional financial support.

The school district has a commitment to all children—the gifted, the average, and the slow learner; the child who has a special interest in music, in art, in literature, in dramatics, in the dance, in mathematics, or in a particular field of science. The school board has a mandate from the people to provide the best possible educational opportunities for all children and youth. It must secure adequate financial support; employ high quality teachers and maintain circumstances in which their capabilities can be used to full advantage; plan, construct, and equip school plants that will house and facilitate the operation of an instructional program; and provide teachers and pupils with the materials and equipment necessary for effective teaching and learning. These are the problems that confront all schools, but particularly schools in the large cities which are attracting such great numbers of people.

The big city has been overtaken by new realities. The basic facts that pertain to the growth and changing character of the big city are well known. But the meaning of these facts is not always clear. The history of this country is being shaped in no small degree by what is taking place in the big cities. And evidence strongly suggests that education is a prime factor in determining whether the big city will satisfy the deep-seated desires of people; develop further as a cultural center; continue as a focal point of economic enterprise with full employment opportunities, rising levels of living, strong institutions, and a better life for the people or whether it will deteriorate; lose its attraction for people, business, and industry; and lead the way into cultural decline.

The ultimate purpose of the city is to provide and sustain a total living environment that has diversity, that allows freedom of choice, that generates rational interaction among people and between them and their surroundings, and that gives people reasonable opportunities to reach the purposes they seek. The city is not a mere physical entity composed of buildings, streets, business places, industries, institutions, and government. The city is people—all people: the strong and the weak, the rich and the poor, the newcomer and the old-timer—not living in isolation but interacting, intermingling, cooperating, and competing as they follow diverse pathways and form different social patterns in seeking their ultimate destinies.

Great and powerful as this country is, it cannot afford waste of human resources, from the standpoint of direct economic considerations, from the standpoint of humanity, or from the standpoint of the fulfillment of the promise of democracy. The schools of the United States, although often themselves suffering from poverty of resources, have always been in the forefront of a "war on poverty." The demographic background of this struggle as it must be conducted in this new era and the implications of present-day economic realities must be understood. Otherwise, the schools will not be as successful as they have been in the past in helping to break the vicious circle of ignorance and poverty.

POPULATION

The United States has grown from 210 settlers in 1610 to 195 million inhabitants in 1965. The handful of these early settlers were perched on the eastern rim of the 3 million square miles later occupied by the 48 states. Today that area has been filled and two new states with an area totaling almost 600,000 square miles have been added. The nation's 210 forebears and their descendants did not accomplish this gigantic task alone. They called on almost all the nations of the earth to help them. Forty-three million immigrants came in answer to the challenge of conquering the mountains and the deserts; taming the wilderness; and spanning the vast territory with trails, rails, roads, and highways. Together, they broke the sod and planted the plains and river valleys. They mined the plentiful underground resources with which the country had been so bountifully blessed by nature. They harnessed the rivers to produce electric power for the factories they constructed. Together they built the richest, strongest, and most productive economy the world has ever known.

On the move. The early settlers, their descendants, and the immigrants who joined them became known as "the people of plenty" and, because so many of them seemed to be constantly on the move, as "those restless Americans." These two labels are intimately related. It was only by uprooting themselves and moving here in the first place that the immigrant ancestors achieved the opportunities which produced wealth. And once here, they and their descendants seldom hesitated to move in search of greater economic opportunities.

The first official accounting of this movement was in the census of 1850. It was then noted that more than one person in every five—21.3 percent, to be exact—was living in a state other than his state of birth. The 1950 and 1960 censuses showed that the proportion had risen closer to one out of four: 23.5 percent in 1950 and 24.8 percent in 1960. The main thrust of the movement was westward. The 1960 count found that 7,416,453 persons born east of the Mississippi River were living west of it. It also showed that 3,571,970 persons born in the West were living in the East. The net gain for the West through the interchange was 3,844,483 persons.[2]

The second major thrust was from south to north. In 1960 there were 6,569,567 persons who were born in the South living in the North. But the net gain to the North was only 2,022,646, since those born in the North but living in the South totaled 4,546,921.

The third major thrust of internal movement has been from rural to urban areas. The urban population of the United States has risen from 5 percent of the total in 1790, when the first census was taken, to 70 percent in 1960—from 202,000 to 125 million. City growth has always involved in-migration, since usually city populations have not reproduced themselves.

Immigration accounted for a sizable proportion of city growth until World War I, when most travel of aliens to the United States was cut off. Drastic restrictions on immigration followed. These two restrictions were followed by the decade of the Great Depression, which resulted in a reduction in migration to cities and a net outflow of immigrants returning to their former homes.

Data on the net annual movement off the farm and to cities [3] for the past four decades show a marked relationship to employment opportunities in the cities:

1920-29	630,000
1930-39	383,000
1940-49	952,000
1950-59	805,000

The reduction in the thirties was due, of course, to the Depression, and in the fifties to the high rate of unemployment prevailing in most industrial centers. City growth through in-migration is not as important today as it was in the forties for two reasons: reduction in employment opportunities (which overwhelmingly are the reasons for migration) and more competition for urban jobs by persons born and raised in the city as a result of the "baby boom" which started in the forties.

Internal migration continues to affect millions of persons, however. People move from city to city, from farm to farm, from farm to city, and from city to farm. People continue to migrate away from areas with less economic opportunity to wherever job possibilities

[2] U.S. Department of Commerce, Bureau of the Census. *U.S. Census of Population: 1960. Subject Reports. State of Birth.* Final Report PC (2)-2A. Washington, D.C.: Government Printing Office, 1963. p. 1.

[3] Shyrock, Henry S., Jr. *Population Mobility Within the United States.* Chicago: Community and Family Study Center, University of Chicago, 1965. pp. 325-26.

exist. Half of the 3,043 counties in the nation lost population in the past decade. Twenty-eight states and the District of Columbia "exported" more persons than they gained from in-migration in the 1950-60 decade. Five states (Iowa, Kentucky, Mississippi, South Carolina, and Tennessee) have experienced net outmigration in every decade since 1880. The main direction of migration is from the interior of the country toward certain sections of the edges—the Pacific Coast, the Gulf Coast, the Middle Atlantic states, and the lower edge of the Great Lakes. These are the areas of greatest economic development.[4]

The result, obtained from state-of-birth data, is a higher rate of migration than ever before recorded by the census. But these data *underestimate* internal migration. Therefore, the Census Bureau began, in 1947, the annual collection of data on both *moving* (technically defined as changing residences within a county) and all other changes of residence, called *migration*. These figures give an even clearer picture of the extent of population mobility. Every year some 30 million persons one year old or over move their homes. Some 20 to 24 million move only within counties, but about 5 million move across county lines; from 5 to 6 million move across at least one state line; and of this latter group, two-thirds move across regional lines.

The cities and the suburbs. The trek toward the cities has been so nearly universal that a survey in 1952 indicated that "one of every three adults living in a nonfarm place was reared on a farm." [5]

There is a fourth thrust of population movement which has important social, economic, and political consequences and which profoundly affects the schools—the surge to the suburbs. The urge to move out of the city to where "the grass is green" is probably as old as urban settlement itself. A Babylonian manuscript quotes a suburban enthusiast who refers to his "little place only a few minutes from the noise and dust of the city, where there is peace, quiet and fresh air." The Romans gave us the word "sub-urbs." The outskirts of Boston became famous through the writings of Emerson and Thoreau during the "flowering of New England." Many other examples could be cited.

Post World War II developments helped to speed up the well-established tendency of persons who had moved up on the economic

---

[4] Bogue, Donald J. "Population Growth in the United States." *The Population Dilemma.* (Edited by Philip M. Hauser.) Englewood Cliffs, N.J.: Prentice-Hall, 1963. pp. 70-93.

[5] Freedman, Ronald, and Freedman, Deborah. "Farm-Reared Elements in the Nonfarm Population." *Rural Sociology* 21: 50; March 1956.

ladder to want to own their own homes. Increased population density in most older cities had resulted in fewer single-family dwellings and more apartment houses. These trends, plus the aging of the city's physical plant, began to raise governmental expenses, particularly in the older areas. Consequently, returning veterans and other qualified people eagerly took advantage of government-backed mortgages ón relatively easy terms to purchase suburban homes. The construction industry rapidly cleared farm land and surburbs mushroomed. Comparative growth rates for central cities and "rings" in the metropolitan areas of the United States since 1900 are revealing:

Percent of population growth inside central cities and outside central cities, 1900-1960 [6]

Period	Inside central city	Outside central city
1900-10	37.1	23.6
1910-20	27.7	20.0
1920-30	24.3	32.3
1930-40	5.6	14.6
1940-50	14.7	35.9
1950-60	10.7	48.5

Slums. The accelerated exodus to the suburbs came at a propitious time. Many of the big cities had grown precipitously as a result of war-time demands for labor. Workers and their families moved into areas already suffering from housing shortages. The suburban movement left some used housing in the central city available for the newcomers, many times as a result of several shifts in its utilization as long-time residents moved into better housing. The result was a residential pattern as old as urban history—the slums serving as a reception area for lower-class newcomers. Here they crowded into dwelling units already old and dilapidated and often paid, in total, rent higher than the original inhabitants had paid. They suffered from inadequate maintenance, from inadequate sanitation and other services, from inadequate community facilities; and, to add insult to injury, they often became the scapegoats and were blamed for the conditions they had inherited and from which they suffered. They were even blamed for uprooting former inhabitants and forcing

[6] U.S. Department of Commerce, Bureau of the Census. *U.S. Census of Population: 1960. Selected Area Reports. Standard Metropolitan Statistical Areas.* Final Report PC (3)-1D. Washington, D.C.: Government Printing Office, 1963. p. 1.

them to move to the suburbs. This circumstance is not unique to American urbanization. Slums have existed in practically all big cities of all countries in the world since the beginning of urbanism.

NEWCOMERS TO THE CITY

Many studies have indicated that farm-reared persons are at a disadvantage in an urban environment. They have almost invariably had less formal education, they are likely to have lower aspiration levels, they have lower-paid and lower-status jobs, and they participate less in both political and voluntary association activities. These generalizations are based on a number of studies which have dealt with native-born white people. These studies show that even with these groups the word *gradual* must be stressed in the definition of integration adopted at the Havana Conference of UNESCO:

> The gradual process by which new residents become active participants in the economic, social, civic, cultural and spiritual affairs of a new homeland.[7]

One could readily predict that newcomers to the city who are more highly visible than the native-born white groups would have even more problems; in fact would come closer to repeating the experiences of the great groups of immigrants who came to the United States during the last part of the nineteenth century and the early part of the twentieth century. Visibility increases, of course, as the personal characteristics of the newcomer differ from those of the receiving population; skin color, language, manner of dress, or conspicuous behavior all affect visibility.

Five relatively large streams of visible migrants are evident in present-day internal migration. They are, in descending order of numerical importance, Negroes, Southern Appalachian mountaineers, Mexican-Americans, Puerto Ricans, and American Indians.

The 20 million Negroes in the United States are now slightly more highly urbanized than the population as a whole. According to the 1960 census, 66.4 percent of the Spanish-surname population in the five Southwestern states which have the heaviest concentrations of people of Mexican or Spanish ancestry live in urban areas; another 21.5 percent of these people live in "rural non-farm" neighborhoods and communities. The 616,000 Puerto Ricans who had by 1960 migrated to the mainland United States live almost entirely in urban areas. On the other hand, most of the 523,000 Indians in

---

[7] Borrie, W. D. *The Cultural Integration of Immigrants.* Paris, France: UNESCO, 1959. pp. 93-94.

the country live in rural areas, but governmental efforts are being made to get them to move to urban areas.

Numerous studies indicate that the newcomer to the city from the farm must bridge a "social distance" gap after he has traversed the geographical distance from his old home to a new one. The more he differs from the receiving population, the greater the gap. This is the major reason for the great similarities and parallels in types of difficulties experienced, as reported from various parts of the country, no matter which "visible" group of newcomers is involved.

Basic to an understanding of them and their problems and to developing programs for helping them is realization that successful urban living involves a variety of patterns of learned behavior. The newcomer must learn, and learn rapidly, how to cope with new and strange problems. Habits learned in different, and usually simpler, surroundings do not lead to satisfactory living in the new environment. Customary ways of making a living, keeping house, raising children, visiting friends and neighbors, playing, and worshipping may all, and all at one time, be called into question. Matters treated casually in the old environment may in the new suddenly become invested with high emotional content; for example, the disposal of refuse and the manner of dress. Added to the difficulties arising from these puzzling changes, there is often reduction in self-esteem which comes from being labelled a "problem"—from being treated as a member of a conspicuous "minority"—instead of as a person.

Most visible migrants share many of the difficulties of the local lower working class. Securing decent housing at reasonable rates is almost invariably the major problem. These migrants are likely to be unskilled or semiskilled and employed in industries subject to seasonal fluctuations and vulnerable to the ups and downs of the business cycle. They are victims of the rule of "last hired, first fired." Their wages are generally low, and thus their ability to save is low.

The lower-class newcomers join, in the slum areas, the strangers in the city who have lived there for years. They are those who have never been allowed to participate as full citizens in civic, economic, social, and political life. They are often as unaccustomed to many of the ways of the city as are the newcomers. Discrimination has crippled their efforts to follow the paths generally trodden by earlier immigrants in moving up the occupational ladder. Even when they have been able to improve their economic status, they often have been denied the right to move to a better neighborhood, to attend the school or church of their choice, to prepare for any vocation to which their ability might admit them, or to practice it if they became prepared. In short, they have not been able to bridge the "social distance" gap even with longer residence. Their frustrations and lack of success are reflected in lower aspiration levels. Numerous studies have showed that aspiration levels usually reflect realistic appraisals of social, economic, and political probabilities.

CHALLENGE TO THE SCHOOLS

The school is the most important institution of the community in helping the newcomer find his place in the city and develop the skills and understandings needed in a way of life considerably different from the life of the community from which he has come. The schools are hampered in this task by a number of factors. One is widespread racial and class residential segregation in the cities. Another is unsatisfactory housing. A social worker discussing housing for newcomers in Cincinnati said, "We are fleecing them in rent. . . . Families shift around trying to find cheaper rent." A place with at least minimal decency in regard to cleanliness, absence of roaches and rodents, and reasonable fire safety is beyond the reach of many low-income families.[8]

The schools are hit particularly hard by high mobility. Big city systems throughout the nation report that many schools have an annual turnover rate approaching 100 percent. In addition, the schools, as well as other youth-serving community agencies, are feeling the results of the "baby boom." This is dramatized by the fact that about one million more young people reached their eighteenth birthdays in 1965 than did in 1964! And each year's group of 18-year-olds from 1966 to 1974 will be larger than that of the previous year. The "baby boom" has in recent years been reflected in the need for new elementary schools and personnel to teach increasing enrollments. High school enrollments will probably increase 30 percent within the next decade, and colleges, already bulging at the seams, will face even greater demands as the wave rolls on.

Unless present trends are reversed in the coming years, there will be more high school dropouts, more teenage marriages, more teenage divorces, and more juvenile delinquency. These results will come from a growing population, even if rates remain constant. As children born during the "baby boom" reach marriageable age and begin raising families, the number of children in the population will increase and new demands will be placed on schools and other community institutions that are already overburdened. The number of

---

[8] *Report of a Workshop on the Southern Mountaineer in Cincinnati.* Cincinnati: Mayor's Friendly Relations Committee and the Social Service Associations of Greater Cincinnati, 1954. 48 pp.

children born annually, about 4 million in 1964, may be expected to rise to about 6 million by 1975 and to about 6.5 million by 1980. The probability is that the population of the United States by the year 2000 will be about 362 million. If the present rate of national increase continues another 65 years beyond that, the population in this country will reach a phenomenal *one billion* persons!

JOB OPPORTUNITIES

The great increase in the teenage population could be faced with less trepidation if plenty of opportunities for employment were available. What is the future of the young people who are just on the verge of entering the labor force? Yesterday's pleasant dreams of a future in which technology would enable man to devote himself to education, recreation, and leisure threaten to become tomorrow's nightmares. Millions today are jobless, millions more are working only part-time, and still others are working far below their highest level of skill. The year 1964 was the fifth consecutive one in which the unemployment rate averaged at least 5 percent; it dropped slightly in 1965. And youth unemployment runs as high as 12 to 15 percent, while unemployment among Negroes is at least twice as high as the national rate. Each of the three business recessions of the past decade has left a larger residue of unemployment. Long-term unemployment (15 weeks or over) increased 100 percent between 1957 and 1962, and very-long-term unemployment (6 months or over) rose about 150 percent.

The private sector of the economy is no longer providing a sufficient number of new jobs as new people pile into the labor force. Between 1947 and 1957, it supplied 700,000 more nonfarm jobs each year, but from 1957 to 1962 the number fell to 175,000 annually. Only the public sector of the economy has showed an increasing rate of job creation since 1957. This growth has been largely in state and local governmental employment, which averaged 185,000 jobs annually between 1947 and 1957. The average for the next five years was 285,000 jobs per year. But the labor force was increasing by over 666,000 per year during that period. It has now risen drastically. During 1965, some 3,700,000 youth reached the age of 18.

The shift in employment has generally been away from those occupations engaging unskilled and semiskilled workers toward those requiring higher levels of skill.[9] More and more, at least a high

[9] Henderson, John P. *Changes in the Industrial Distribution of Employment, 1919-1959.* University of Illinois Bulletin, Vol. 59, No. 3. Urbana: University of Illinois, August 1961. 104 pp.

school diploma is a requirement for almost any job. Professional and technical workers, of course, require at least four years of college. Unemployment increased between 1950 and 1959 for every group of workers except those with 13 years or more of schooling. School systems must exert ever greater efforts to make education more meaningful in the era of automation. The threat of machines' becoming Frankensteins may otherwise become more than a literary allusion.

The need for jobs—or alternative sources of income—is desperate for the 35 million people who live in poverty.

> *Racial discrimination* must be eliminated. Programs to help economically depressed members of racial minority groups gain new skills will benefit little if employment opportunity is still blocked by discrimination.[10]

The biggest single group of the poverty-stricken is the biggest single "visible" minority—the Negroes. Forty percent of them live in poverty. Special efforts are required on the part of school systems and all other community agencies to overcome the terrible heritage of 250 years of slavery and 100 years of technical freedom marred and often almost totally destroyed by discrimination. Although education "pays" for the Negro, it still leaves him behind the white man. The same occupation, with the same educational requirements, still pays the Negro less than the white man. "In most occupations, nonwhite men earned about three-fourths as much as whites with the same amount of schooling," according to census income expert Herman P. Miller.[11]

Overall, lifetime earnings of Negro men, according to 1960 census data, were only about two-thirds those of white men. Current earnings for Negro men in 1959 were 60 percent of white male earnings; Negro women averaged 50.3 percent of the earnings of white women. There does not appear to have been any improvement since 1960. Unemployment rates, occupation by occupation and industry by industry, are much higher for Negroes than for whites. The proportion of long-term and very-long-term unemployed Negro males is about one-third higher than that of white males; of Negro females, about one-fourth higher.

---

[10] Johnson, Lyndon B. "Manpower Report of the President." *Manpower Report of the President and a Report on Manpower Requirements, Resources, Utilization, and Training by the United States Department of Labor.* Washington, D.C.: Government Printing Office, March 1964. p. XVIII.

[11] Miller, Herman P. *Rich Man, Poor Man: The Distribution of Income in America.* New York: Thomas Y. Crowell Co., 1964. p. 152.

The most disadvantaged group in the country, the American Indians, had an unemployment rate of 14.5 percent in 1960, compared to 5.1 for the total population; on some reservations the rate was very much higher. The median 1959 income of Indian men was $2,300 below that of all men in the population and lower than that of any other disadvantaged group.

Puerto Ricans and Mexican-Americans have common problems of low educational attainment and language barriers, high rates of unemployment, and low incomes. They are also handicapped by discrimination in employment in New York and other cities where Puerto Ricans are concentrated, and in the Southwest, where most Mexican-Americans are located.

In 1960 the unemployment rate for Puerto Rican workers was 10 percent and for Mexican-Americans 8.3 percent, compared with 5.1 percent for the total civilian labor force.[12]

THE ROLE OF THE SCHOOL

The schools for decades have performed the two major functions of helping orient the newcomer and helping the receiving community understand and accept him. Often people in the community have never formally acknowledged that the schools should do the job that needs to be done. In fact, many citizens of the receiving community have not even realized that there is a job to be done.

One task of the schools is to help the whole community know and understand the newcomer. This is only part of the school's task in helping to raise a generation of young people who can cope with a world where the ethnocentrism which has so long cursed humanity will yield to the rule of reason, where change is taken in stride instead of being feared, and where the high ethical ideals of the world's greatest thinkers will become meaningful in daily life. Unless an accepting, understanding climate is created in the receiving community, other problems will arise and the task of the schools will be immeasurably more difficult.

That major task is to teach the newcomer and his children the ways of life in the big city or the smaller community to which he has come. Most newcomers do move into the big cities. Here, life is complicated for everyone, especially for the newcomer, by the presence of so many styles of life. The "melting pot" approach to

---

[12] Wirtz, W. Willard. "Report on Manpower Requirements, Resources, Utilization, and Training by the United States Department of Labor." *Manpower Report of the President and a Report on Manpower Requirements, Resources, Utilization, and Training by the United States Department of Labor.* Washington, D.C.: Government Printing Office, 1964. p. 7.

immigrant education that attempted to shame the newcomer into repudiating his cultural background, "forgetting the old country," and discarding the mother tongue and its songs and its poems deprived the receiving community of rich cultural potential and often frustrated rather than helped its new citizens. Such an approach to assimilating newcomers into a new cultural setting is as out-of-date as the surrey with the fringe on top.

While most teachers and administrators have wholesome attitudes toward what some persons patronizingly call the "culturally deprived" child, others act as though the second word in that label should be spelled with an *a* and the modifier dropped. The Educational Policies Commission report *Education and the Disadvantaged American* puts the matter succinctly:

> Despite their better judgment, people of another background often feel that disadvantaged children are by nature perverse, vulgar, or lazy. Children sense quickly the attitudes of school people toward them, and they retaliate against condescension or intolerance with hostility, absenteeism, and failure.[13]

The middle class culture of the teacher provides him with an ethnocentric outlook unless preservice or inservice training through anthropology, sociology, and up-to-date psychology has broadened his outlook and increased his understanding of people with cultural backgrounds different from his own. Unfortunately, outdated psychology reflected in many so-called "intelligence" tests tends to buttress and confirm teachers' prejudices.

Actually, in contacts with culturally different persons, it is the inadequacy of one's own culture which is being exposed. But many times it is much more comfortable to blame the newcomer than to question and change established programs—to put one's own house in order. History clearly shows that both the culture and the economy of the United States have been strengthened by acceptance of the cultural traits of the strangers who came to live in its cities and towns and open country places.

The very existence of the democratic way of life and especially of the promise it holds for the two-thirds of the peoples of the world who are colored will be called into question if nonwhite fellow citizens are unable to participate in full measure in American society. The schools must play a key role in bringing about that participation.

There are millions of disadvantaged persons moving from small towns and open country places into the great urban centers. The

---

[13] National Education Association and American Association of School Administrators, Educational Policies Commission. *Education and the Disadvantaged American.* Washington, D.C.: the Commission, 1962. p. 19.

school must not shirk its duty of helping bring them into the mainstream of civic, economic, and social life. Neither the school nor active and conscientious citizens can be satisfied with the high-level abstractions which contend that "nothing can be done" to help culturally different youngsters from disadvantaged areas. School and community programs have produced impressive gains in so-called IQs, in reading ability, in reduction of rowdyism and vandalism, and in the holding power of schools.

Finally, a tremendous weight of the past must be sloughed off—the concept that the purpose of the school is to *adjust* the child to the "realities" of his existence. A "contented cow" may well be an appealing symbol for milk products, but it has no place in any symbolism for education in the world today. No educator with high ideals can ask his pupils to "adjust" to slum living. Slums must be wiped out.

If society is to meet and solve the problems faced today, school systems must become active, not passive—innovative, not imitative. They must enlist and utilize the full educational potential of the entire community. A truly affluent society in which each citizen is not only permitted but encouraged to develop his potentialities to their fullest realization will be built only through more active participation of the entire citizenry—teachers, administrators, parents, and young people themselves.

IMPERATIVE

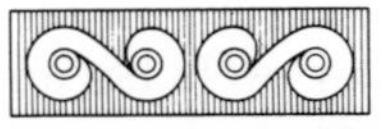

3 · TO PREPARE PEOPLE FOR THE WORLD OF WORK

The forces that affect and shape men's lives, that determine how and to what extent they get along in the world, have become highly complicated, technical, rapidly moving, and efficient. They demand high degrees of skill, alertness, and understanding. If these new and powerful forces are to be harnessed and managed to the best interests of all people, integrity and high purpose must be deeply imbedded in the commitments and the actions of all people. Perhaps the greatest challenge in this new age is to learn how to manage the creatures of inventive genius rather than let them become unmanageable forces that crush the lives and spirits of great groups of people.

The United States was founded and has been developed on the basic premise that everybody is important—that everybody has a contribution to make and is entitled to a fighting chance to develop the best that is in him. Now great groups of people find themselves in circumstances where forces beyond their control overpower them and crush them—deal them out.

The hopes, goals, and beliefs of people today, as in all past history, are shaped in great measure by the life about them—by the circumstances in which they live and try to get along in the world. The deep-seated and almost universal desires of people to get along in the world include—

Food to appease hunger

Clothing and shelter for comfort

A home and family

A job that claims the approbation of one's associates

A measure of self-respect

Compatible relationships with other people

A chance to be somebody of worth, importance, and dignity.

This decade is marked by rapid change and specialization. Each accelerates the other. Increased productivity—getting the job done more quickly and economically—is the key to industrial and commercial success. At times this objective is achieved at the expense of the individual whose knowledge no longer applies and whose skills are no longer needed. Because of haste to produce, some individuals have become expendable. When unemployed, they lose purchasing power, and the total economy suffers, with widespread loss of personal income.

The nagging specter of unemployment is one of the most troublesome problems facing society, in spite of the fact that apparently there are unfilled manpower needs. Current estimates place the number of unemployed persons in the neighborhood of 4 million and the unemployment rate close to 5 percent.

It is inevitable during a period of change and specialization that job requirements become more complex, calling for a higher level of problem-solving ability. The worker who does not keep abreast through training and education soon falls by the wayside. He must anticipate new demands on his talents and prepare for them to avoid becoming expendable. *It is imperative that the school be ready to assist him and to lead the way in meeting new manpower needs.*

In today's market, there is less and less opportunity for the unskilled laborer and the untrained adolescent. Of particular concern are the 1 million unemployed youth under the age of 24. These are youngsters who possess no salable skills and who spend their days in idleness and despair at a time in their lives when proper work habits and attitudes should be in the process of formation. In their present status they are the rejects of the society that produced them.

Unless something is done, this horde of unwanted young men and women will grow larger. During the next 10 years there will be 30 million new workers looking for jobs. Two to three million will have no more than a grade school education. Seven and a half million will be without a high school diploma. Thirty-five percent of those who enter high school will not graduate. Can a free society survive when one-third of its young people have but little hope of sharing in the abundance of the nation?

In the broadest definition of its usefulness to society, therefore, *it is imperative that the school be organized to help the worker make successful career changes and to assist young people in preparing for the world of work.* Every school system must increase its productivity and reduce the time lag between the facts of change and reeducation for it. Educators must be aware of the need for the production of highly flexible, versatile manpower which can retool itself quickly when swift changes make previous education and experience obsolete. It is frequently said, "If we are doing it now, it's obsolete." This may be an exaggeration, but this tersely stated idea highlights the necessity for revitalizing and updating that segment of the educational program primarily concerned with preparation for the world of work.

It is highly probable that within the next 20 years, much of the making of an automobile, the packaging of food, and inventory of stock will be programed by data-processing machines and done by automated machinery. Repetitive labor, as such, will be largely a fact of the past. The familiar pyramidal occupational classification with unskilled labor constituting the broad base and the professions at the top will be replaced by a barrel-like pattern of distribution with small ends and a bulging center in which substantial educational attainments are required. There will be more button pushing, more replacement than repair, and greater emphasis—so far as human beings are concerned—upon management and distribution. The human touch may disappear even in paper work and be replaced by automation. Priority will be given to the production of devices which, once operating, may assume greater importance in the routine processes of production than the individuals they replace. The only limits to modern technology are the mind and the will of man.

The rapidity with which the federal government has entered into partnership with state and local communities in educational matters is evidence of the increasing importance national leaders attach to the relationship between well-prepared workers and the health of the national economy. Proof exists in the Vocational Education Act of 1963, the Manpower Development and Training Act, the Economic Opportunity Act, the National Defense Education Act, and the recently passed Elementary and Secondary Education Act of 1965—all introduced into and approved by the Congress in a remarkably short time.

These actions at the federal level suggest that the schools either have been derelict in making needed changes or have failed to see the importance of training for vocational competence and flexibility. To no small extent, failure of states and local communities to provide the necessary financial support for an increasingly complex educational structure has been a distinct handicap. There is real danger that failure on the part of local and state school authorities to prepare young people for the ever-changing world of work may result in loss of control of this responsibility to other agencies.

It is imperative that in the years ahead there be more education for the individual. The average level of education completed by pupils after World War I was slightly above grade 8 and after World War II, grade 10. Currently, the average level completed is moving up toward grade 12. It is not unrealistic to expect that in the near future, 14 years of basic education for all will become the norm of society.

Some time during the last 6 years of schoolwork, young people must prepare for their initial working experience. Thirty-five percent of their waking hours will be spent at making a living. No other part of man's activities so completely influences his way of life.

For these reasons, *it is imperative that general education at all levels be strengthened; that vocational education be related more realistically to a rapidly changing world of work; and that much more time, skill, and money be devoted to vocational guidance in schools at all levels and through agencies and institutions in the community.*

VOCATIONAL EDUCATION IN THE YEARS AHEAD

It is imperative that dignity be attached to all socially useful labor. One of the first obligations of educators is to raise the prestige of all socially useful labor and to place education for the professions in its proper perspective. At the outside, only 12 in every 100 individuals in the average community will find their occupational futures in medicine, law, teaching, nursing, dietetics, engineering, or other professions. Citizens and parents must come to realize that over 80 percent of the young people entering the labor market will be needed in occupations other than the professions. While particular prestige has been attached to education for the professions and related occupations, other equally important vocations have been given somewhat lower priority and less attention.

Right now this country stands at the threshold of a breakthrough in the appreciation of all kinds of learning. Increased remuneration to graduates in the trades and those entering industry below the professional level has helped to improve the prestige of those preferring or having to work in occupations other than the professions. Schools can do a great deal to accelerate this movement. Teachers, of all people, ought to applaud publicly and often the contributions all types of labor make to a successful nation. Modern, up-to-date housing for vocational education can improve the image of the man who works with his hands.

Simple steps that can be taken in any community to enhance the status of jobs outside the professions include public exhibits of products made by students, awards for vocational excellence, recognition of successful adult artisans in school assemblies and at other school functions, and singling out for attention pupils who are outstanding in vocational training. The ideal is reached when young people are made conscious of the dignity of all honorable labor and learn that it takes teamwork to achieve industrial and social goals.

Recently, after a play had been presented in a school assembly, the audience from the community insisted on curtain call after curtain call for the leading actor. After several of them, the young Barrymore induced the stage crew to appear with him. He said, "Perhaps I can act a bit, but without those who work behind the scenes, no production of this kind could be possible." This is the attitude that must be created among young people and adults as well.

FROM THE GENERAL TO THE SPECIFIC

The more specific the vocational training of an individual, the more vulnerable he is to changes in employment opportunities over which he has little or no control. The vocational education program for tomorrow must be directed toward general vocational excellence in broad occupational areas, leaving to the specific industry or craft the obligation of training workers for their particular assignments. The nearer the individual is to his clearly identified and realistic vocational goal, the more specific his preparation ought to be. The potential doctor of medicine takes biology and chemistry in high school, biochemistry in college, and general medicine in his early years of graduate school; he begins to specialize as he comes closer to the practice of medicine. The electronics specialist begins with exploratory industrial arts before entering upon the more complicated operations of layout, design, and circuits. The dietician's first educational experiences are in the preparation of foods and cooking; later the more complex studies of nutrition and dietetics are undertaken. The high school trained agriculturist will have explored botany, chemistry, zoology, and physics before undertaking the specifics of crop rotation, dairy operations, or machine farming.

These progressions suggest a need for careful synchronization of transition from the general to the specific, from background instruction to practice, apprenticeship, and application. Subjects, courses, and activities must be carefully tailored to give sequence and meaning to the entire training process and to enable the individual to see the relationship of each step to his ultimate goal. Enough practical application to whet the student's appetite must be interwoven with general preparation and background information. Learning how to measure with a 6-foot rule is relatively meaningless unless one has practice in measuring for a particular purpose.

It is imperative that development of attitudes toward and experiences in vocational education begin early and be continual.

PRESCHOOL EXPERIENCES

The preschool child can be assigned simple tasks around the house, in nursery school, in Sunday school, in the neighborhood, and—with obvious limitations—in the community. There is evidence that patterns of behavior and attitudes begin to form much earlier than was once thought. The preschool period is also the time to attempt to compensate for cultural deficiencies—deficiencies which have significance in job choice. Activities in nursery school, prekindergarten, and kindergarten have great importance. Operation Head Start, one of the programs developed under the Economic Opportunity Act of 1964, suggests increasing concern for beginning early to develop positive attitudes toward school, self, and work habits.

ELEMENTARY SCHOOL

Although specific preparation for occupational excellence is not a proper goal of the elementary school, the foundations for vocational preparation can and should be laid at this level. Children must be taught to read, to compute, to analyze, and to acquire factual information. These skills are essential to vocational proficiency and other activities, and they can be taught with deliberate reference to the vocations.

The elementary school should provide some opportunity for pupil display of interests other than those related to general academic or college preparatory subjects. Art, drawing, industrial arts, and homemaking offer excellent exploratory experiences. The school's cumulative record should contain evidence of individual abilities and interests. The reading program should contain material about people at work, simple biographies, and information about jobs. The Rochester Reading Series, developed in Rochester, New York, and now produced by Science Research Associates, is a fine example of how children are taught to read while attention is focused on common occupations. Children like learning from real-life situations. When they can observe as they read, their reading improves. At the same time, they acquire useful information about vocations.

The mental health film *The Passion for Life* is a good example of integrating the commonly accepted goals of school with an analysis of the work people do and why and of what their preparation has to be. One can only wish curriculum organizers, textbook writers, and teachers could catch the importance of attaching real meaning to classroom situations and use the techniques suggested in this exciting film.

SECONDARY SCHOOL

Much of what has been said of the need for focusing attention on vocations in the elementary school applies equally well to junior and senior high schools. In addition, junior and senior high schools have major responsibilities for providing counseling and exploratory experiences.

Traditional academic education is neither meaningful nor productive for a substantial number of young people. The school must, of course, help these young people to be literate and enable them to compete with others who have more and different talents. But, obviously, one of their greatest needs is to develop salable skills. Work experience and short unit occupational education are badly needed for a substantial number of pupils.

Schools should give credit for work experience and stimulate business and industry to assist in such programs. The school itself can become a laboratory. Classroom, library, audiovisual headquarters, cafeteria, and traffic control can provide experiences that encourage young people to be dependable and accurate and to use good judgment. With appropriate supervision they can be taught to work with others, to take criticism, and to attach accurate values to success and failure. The question of pay for such character-building training is irrelevant. The youngster who leaves high school must take with him positive attitudes, work habits, and social behavior. Failure on the job usually is caused not so much by lack of working skill or knowledge as by lack of suitable personal characteristics, proper attitudes, and work habits essential for job success. The decrease in opportunities for young people to acquire these habits in the home and in industry makes it essential that the school provide work experiences in the curriculum.

The business education program of the modern comprehensive high school has achieved prestige and importance for the youngster who intends to enter the job market immediately after graduation. Business education leaders have been instrumental in modernizing their program in such areas as distributive education, cooperative office practice, data processing, use of office machines, and machine bookkeeping. This process must be accelerated to keep pace with the rapidity of change in business operation.

The comprehensive high school provides training, either in a separate school or within its own walls, for the crafts, trades, and service occupations. The variety of courses offered and their direction are dependent on the labor needs of the immediate community. Variation is much more probable in large urban areas than it is in rural areas. Vocational opportunities in regional high schools should make it possible for youth from small-town high schools to achieve vocational goals. Other possibilities for teaching youth from relatively isolated areas include correspondence courses, educational television, summer programs, telephone classes, and individualized credit seminars. Certainly boys and girls should not be penalized because of the geographic location of their residences.

THE INDUSTRIAL-VOCATIONAL-TECHNICAL HIGH SCHOOL

The industrial-vocational-technical high school prepares young people for various occupations. This three-way terminology suggests the confusion that has existed in identifying this type of high school. Undoubtedly, all three adjectives apply in varying degrees, depending on the location of the school and local occupational possibilities. Shopwork and related programs are geared to specific job placement. Study of occupational needs is a prerequisite to curriculum organization, and each school must be able to react almost immediately to changes in occupational requirements.

A program of research is needed to identify factors that correlate high potential with shop success and success on the job. Specific criteria for entrance into the various vocational training areas must be developed, and most aptitude tests are not too helpful. Expressed, sustained interest has some merit as a means of identifying potentially successful students. The ability to compute and to read are still fairly good predictions of later shop success, as are marks in industrial arts and drafting.

Most offerings of the four-year technical-industrial-vocational high school are bound to become increasingly complex. Higher pupil performance will be required. The vocational school must become increasingly selective. Requirements for specific job areas must be refined.

There is a need to relate intake of numbers of students to job opportunities. Although increased mobility greatly extends the range of employment opportunities, a substantial percentage of youth graduating from high school tend to remain in the region in which they were born or to return to it after relatively brief absences. Under these circumstances, it would be as absurd for the vocational high school of the North to prepare youth for the turpentine industry of the South as to prepare youth in the South for the watchmaking industry of New England. The vigilant vocational school will be aware of the job picture nationally but will realistically concern itself with preparation for job opportunities in the region it serves.

American people have good reason for considerable pride in their educational buildings; but unfortunately, such pride has overlooked facilities for vocational education. In far too many instances, vocational programs have been housed in cast-off elementary or secondary schools, in basements, or in temporary quarters in a run-down section of the neighborhood. It is high time that preparation for occupational life be dignified with facilities specifically constructed for this purpose and equal in quality to facilities for every other segment of the comprehensive program. Buildings must be flexible and capable of almost instantaneous change. Equipment must be modern and up-to-date.

The vocational school should not be expected to do more than meet its objectives. All too frequently, the vocational school has been considered a panacea for dropouts. Vocational schools at times have been established to meet specific labor shortages. Where this has been the case, there has been a tendency for pupils to drop out of school as soon as salable skills have been developed.

Vocational schools have not been equated with the importance of the occupations they serve, nor have they been adequately financed. Vocational schools are expensive to equip. Instruction must be individualized to a considerable degree. Consequently, classes must be kept small.

The Vocational Education Act of 1963 (Public Law 88-210) subsidizes existing programs and supports new ones so that persons of all ages in all communities of the state will have ready access to vocational training or retraining. This has removed and continues to remove some of the obstacles of finance. It will not remove the greatest deterrent to meeting the vocational needs of youth: unwillingness of people—teachers, administrators, and the general public—to discontinue outdated vocational programs and to develop new ones.

THE COMMUNITY COLLEGE

Two-year academic and technical programs beyond high school have flourished in recent years. The number of high school graduates continues to increase, and as the need for more basic general education is felt, the community college must accept a larger role in vocational education, particularly in semiprofessional, technical, and professional-support occupations. The function of this institution is not duplication of the general education found in the first two years of a four-year liberal arts program. Its unique role is the preparation of youth for entrance into specific jobs in such occupational areas as nursing, accounting, data processing, instrumentation, food technology, agribusiness, psychometry, junior welfare, photography, specification writing, electronics, and the like.

The junior college or community college, a two-year college that draws its students from the immediate geographical area, can and should base its occupational offerings upon the needs of industry, business, and commerce of the region. Thus the Rochester Institute of Technology in New York concentrates upon machine technology, photographic education, and clothing and retail distribution. Phoenix College in Arizona emphasizes electronics, data processing, and medical technology.

The evening division of the community college is of no less importance, since it serves those for whom additional vocational aspirations have not been realized or those needing retraining for new jobs. Here, too, the emphasis in curriculum depends upon the results of occupational demand studies.

COLLEGES AND UNIVERSITIES

Colleges and universities do not list vocational preparedness as a major goal. Nevertheless, what the college or university does and how well the student responds do have a relationship to vocational competency. Traditionally those who are responsible for leadership in colleges and universities shy away from the term *vocational*. They refer to training the mind, molding the intellect, developing critical faculties, general education, and preparation for graduate studies. But the students in universities, as well as in other educational institutions, are deeply concerned about such questions as, What will I do when I graduate? Where can I get the greatest return on my investment? What pursuit will give me the greatest satisfaction in my lifework?

It is time that colleges and universities fully recognize the relationship between collegiate study and vocational success. Without detracting from or minimizing in any respect the great importance of academic learning or learning for its own sake, college and university programs can be materially strengthened by helping students clearly understand how the subject under discussion finds expression in the world of work and in the life about them. This is not for a moment intended to absolve the liberal arts college, the general college, or the university from its commonly accepted responsibilities. It is rather to enrich the cultural and liberalizing experiences it offers by relating them to the practical and the vocational.

ADULT VOCATIONAL EDUCATION

It is imperative that adult vocational education programs be expanded and improved. Major responsibility for the adult vocational education program needed to keep mature workers abreast of changing demands in the labor market should be assigned to public high schools, junior colleges, and colleges and universities; but some responsibility for the adult program should be carried by employers and by community agencies other than the schools and colleges.

Adult vocational education is always expensive; it is even more expensive when it is uncoordinated. The hard facts of economics make it undesirable, if not impractical, for each institution to go its own way in developing and supporting adult vocational education programs. Cooperation on a regional basis that will coordinate efforts, synchronize training, and eliminate overlapping will go a long way in improving educational opportunities for adults and in making efficient use of available resources. The term *region* rather than *state* is deliberately used to emphasize the need for broad approaches to vocational planning. Comprehensive planning should not be restricted or inhibited by state boundaries. To illustrate, the Connecticut River divides Vermont and New Hampshire, but the economic area includes both sides of the river.

It is important that vocational education plants be readily accessible to people who need the training. This may call for several facilities in large urban centers such as Buffalo, New York; Los Angeles, California; and St. Louis, Missouri; or for facilities covering large portions of a state, such as exist in Connecticut, New Hampshire, and New

Jersey. It may even call for centers in industrial plants where the people are working.

A steady stream of data pertinent to changes in occupational opportunities should flow into the adult vocational education program so that the school can anticipate change and adapt the program to newly emerging needs and circumstances. At times it may be necessary for the school to retool its program and change its content almost instantly.

Like all other facets of instruction, the adult vocational education program can never be much better than the quality of the instructors. Herein lies one of the most difficult administrative problems. Individuals who know their trade, craft, or occupation, and who at the same time possess the rare quality of being able to transmit what they know to others in a manner that will help them learn are hard to find. Some administrators are coming to believe that a team approach, pairing a skilled craftsman with an effective teacher, should be made.

The cost of adult vocational education should be a shared responsibility. Industry should bear a share of the expense; the individual should contribute his share; and society, either through the public schools or colleges or through the government, should contribute its share. The end result will be more adequately trained personnel, less unemployment, and fewer people on public relief rolls. It is apparent that the contributions of the underprivileged and the unemployed to the adult vocational education program will be limited to their own time and effort.

Under the provisions of the Manpower Development and Training Act, an experimental program supported by the federal government for the retraining of unemployed individuals has been launched. This program, in addition to bearing the cost of instruction, provides training allowances and travel subsistence for people involved in the program. It is an interesting experiment which has its proponents as well as its critics. In one area, approximately 75 percent of those who entered the program completed their training; 79 percent of these were placed and are still on the job a year later.

VOCATIONAL GUIDANCE

It is imperative that programs of vocational guidance be extended and improved. If vocational education is to be effective, it is essential that students as well as teachers and administrators be fully aware of the training and education needed and that expert analyses of individual abilities and interests be made to assist trainees in making intelligent choices.

Educational guidance in the schools and colleges of this country has generally been better than vocational guidance; yet they are inseparable. They are but two dimensions of the same function. Attempts to help young people understand the process of choosing and entering an occupation have frequently been haphazard or incidental and sometimes completely lacking. Much has been left to chance.

Helping a young person select an area of employment in which he is likely to have reasonable success makes learning significant, adds meaning to subjects taken, and gives purpose to many school and college activities. Proper job placement contributes to mental and physical health and increases the individual's productivity. No other activity undertaken during waking hours occupies more time or so affects total well-being, determines companions, or sets the backdrop for activities as does the occupation the individual chooses to enter. Furthermore, the search for a personal place in a chosen vocation so enriches understanding of occupational conditions that tolerance of other people and other vocations is increased.

It would be a serious mistake to assume that any person makes only one job choice. The rapidity of occupational change, the mobility of people, and the ingenuity of America almost require the average person to plan for a number of jobs. There are the exploratory jobs, the first attempts at lifework, the inevitable changes, the promotions, and possibly an entirely different experience after formal retirement. This emphasizes the need for adult counseling centers. An individual who enters the labor market for the first time in the next decade may find it necessary to make as many as six major changes of occupation during his lifetime. Women prepare for and enter a beginning job, leave it when they are chosen for careers in the home, only to reappear in the job market after their children are grown, when unusual opportunity beckons, or when some catastrophe strikes the male wage earner or others in the family. Mechanization of the home leaves many women with time on their hands which leads them to seek outlets for restless energy. Thus, the woman, too, must think beyond the single job concept.

It is imperative that the vocational guidance program provide young people with a process of self-evaluation to help them make intelligent choices. To help each student to come to know himself, to study the world of work and of job opportunities, to gain experience in matching himself with job possibilities, to discern whether he has the ability to profit from the training involved, and to master the mechanics of getting and holding a job is a clear purpose of the school. A major goal of institutions of learning at all levels is to prepare properly motivated and highly skilled workers enthusiastically devoting a major part of their time, effort, and thought to productive work. This all-important end cannot and must not be left to chance or be merely an incidental by-product of the educative process. The school must not only see this as a major purpose, it must be willing to do something about it. The requirements are—

1. A more direct focus of curriculum upon vocational objectives
2. Opportunity for young people to know themselves
3. Expert counseling
4. Appropriate school-maintained records.

At one time, serious effort was made to include courses in occupations in junior and senior high schools. Unfortunately, much of the written and graphic material for the courses was already out-of-date by the time it reached the classroom. The courses were often taught by uninterested teachers either on a one-period-a-week basis or in the homerooms. Students did not see any worthwhile purpose in the course offering. Occupational information was treated as something to be absorbed—a sort of pouring out of facts and statistics—lacking cohesion and interpretation. Fortunately, administrators and teachers have discovered that the presentation of vocational information must be interwoven with the individual's understanding of himself. Taught in this way, the student comes to see his occupational future in the light of his own assessment of his personal goals, ambitions, abilities, and interests. Every adolescent is concerned about himself—what he is, how he compares, where his talents lie, what he should do about failure, and how he can gain acceptance and recognition.

Several communities are developing courses in "career planning," in which emphasis is placed on learning to guide oneself, learning a procedure, and learning a series of steps which will help the individual to make his choice or choices in an ever-changing vocational world. This approach recognizes that as the world of work changes, so do individuals.

There are at least two levels where such programs should be scheduled. First, at the end of junior high school, grade 9, when senior high school subjects should be chosen in light of vocational goals; and, second, toward the end of high school, when significant decisions must again be made. These promising programs will not be successful unless appropriate prestige is attached to them and teachers are specifically prepared to teach them.

Teachers should help their pupils understand the vocational and disciplinary implications, as well as the educational and cultural values, of every unit of school subject matter. By and large, teachers do well in explaining the educational and cultural aspects of subject matter. They do not do as well with what might be termed the practical, the vocational, and the disciplinary values. The intelligent, practical-minded teacher of physics needs to explain as a first step in the introduction of a new unit what it means to vocational opportunities. The principle of the lever, for one example, has any number of practical applications in the trades, the crafts, and the professions. The teacher who helps students relate the elements in a particular subject to comparable elements in another subject matter field or to life's activities is laying the foundation for transfer of concepts of instruction that may be useful in later life in building masonry walls, connecting wires on a telephone pole, shingling a roof, or engaging in numerous other occupations that call for following precise directions.

Revision of the curriculum of the secondary school is another positive approach to improving vocational education. The present pattern of required and elective subjects, of majors and minors, assumes that the individual has within him the power to integrate subject matter, to see its relationships, and to acquire depth in learning. Curriculum planners should examine present offerings of high schools and explore the possibilities of different subject matter organization. The late W. W. Charters, professor of education at Ohio State University, once said in a convocation that the subject matter of the secondary school at that time would someday become peripheral and that what was then thought of as peripheral would become basic. When asked for further clarification of these basic curricular offerings of the future, he included the study of man, his personality and development; the study of society and group living; and the study of occupations and how to live a rich and satisfying life. He suggested postponement of much subject matter until a student could see purpose in his life and the direction his talents and interests would take as a result of studying himself in relationship to available opportunity.

OPPORTUNITIES TO KNOW THEMSELVES

The right man in the right job is more than chance, although chance does play a part. Increasingly, as the child matures, he acquires insights into his own abilities and interests, attitudes and habits. He accepts the fact that he will not do everything equally well. He knows he must be good at something. He builds a career upon his strong points. He cannot afford to select a vocation which calls for attributes in which he has less than average ability. There is too little time.

Individuals with superior abilities tend, with training and experience, to widen the distance between themselves and those who are average. It is therefore important that the educative process help reveal to each individual the fields of work in which he can be most successful.

The curriculum should be not only a means of acquiring knowledge but a way to get clues to occupational possibilities. Subjects taken, if properly taught, become a means by which individuals discover something of themselves and their interests. The curriculum of the modern school and college can point out the relationship between successful classroom performance and occupational demands. Thus, the school program becomes a screening process through which the student is able, in part, to determine where he is most likely to succeed.

School marks—subjective as they frequently are—are one of the best indexes available of the student's total achievement: his knowledge, skills, attitudes, work habits, and interests. They should be used for prediction as well as for measurement of past accomplishment. Aptitude tests have been used to good advantage in counseling and vocational guidance, but many people, misled by popular articles, tend to place too much credence on the predictive qualities of aptitude tests. No test predicts accurately, and the relationship of test results to predicted job success has not been well established by research. For this reason, all test results must be used with caution.

There is no shortcut to self-discovery. It is a long-term process. It involves extensive experience, exploration, reading about occupations and the biographies of successful men and women; it involves trial and error and the chance to confer with well-informed and well-trained counselors. Because of the complexity of the problem of self-discovery, vocational guidance laboratories staffed by competent occupational specialists should be established in high schools. Here students try out, on a sampling basis, a variety of activities in major occupational fields.

EXPERT COUNSELING SERVICE

Finding the right man for the right job is so important in a country which requires excellence for its survival that no program of community education is complete without adequate counseling services for the students in its schools and its colleges and for the adult population. The problem is so vast, the opportunities so unlimited, and individual abilities so diverse in this era of specialization that this responsibility must be assigned to well qualified personnel—individuals who work well with people, who are skilled in interviewing, and who have the ability to marshal forces in the community necessary to sustain an effective counseling program.

The counselor is a newcomer in the field of professional education. Institutes for training counselors, sponsored by the National Defense Education Act, have accelerated the movement toward better preparation and inservice training for counselors. The case load of the counselor is important. Little can be accomplished if from 400 to 500 pupils have to compete for his attention and time. James Conant, in *The American High School Today,* recommended a case load of 200 to 300 students. If this recommendation were adopted, it would be a marked improvement over what generally prevails, but even this ratio should be reduced.

The existence of trained counselors in the high school does not release teachers from their responsibility for incidental counseling. Group discussion of vocational problems common to almost every student will do much to lighten the load of the busy counselor and provide better guidance services for students.

RECORD KEEPING

The threads of development for a large number of students cannot be kept straight and running on true course without efficiently maintained records. The accomplishments of students, their ambitions, their hopes and aspirations, and their frustrations and disappointments are but a few of the essential data that must be recorded and readily available to the counselor as he works individually with students. The time of a counselor is far too valuable to be spent in the tedious, time-consuming processes of recording such data by hand and in reviewing folders of material to retrieve it when needed. Data can be electronically recorded and made readily available when needed. If the school system is too small to provide this service independently, it can be made available on a regional basis. In larger systems, it may be possible to provide such services on a district basis or even in particular schools in modified form. The important point is that essential records should be maintained and the information should be in form for immediate use.

COMMUNITY MOBILIZATION

The school cannot, by itself, direct, influence, and provide vocational guidance and vocational education. The work of the school program must be enhanced by the support of other institutions and agencies and by many individuals not directly connected with the school system.

The role of the parent. Regardless of statements to the contrary, parents still greatly influence the thinking of their children. To help them in discussing educational goals and vocational aspirations with their children, parents need up-to-date and reliable information. The school can well afford to conduct clinics with parents on the subject of vocational orientation, choice, and preparation as well as to support a parent education program. To date, too much of the parents' role in the vocational orientation of their children has been left to chance.

The role of industry and business. Industry and education need to cooperate in many ways, but particularly in introducing the young learner into the workings of industry. It is the responsibility of the school to clearly state its position with respect to education and training and to disseminate this information to representatives of business, industry, and service agencies. Industry and business must provide general information to the school on the types of jobs available, career openings, and promotion policies. In some instances, they provide tryout opportunities for students who have matured sufficiently. In other instances, equipment, machines, and expendable supplies are provided on a lend-lease basis in order that students be given up-to-date training.

It is important that teachers of vocational subjects have the advice and counsel of business and industrial leaders. Vocational advisory committees should be established and periodical meetings scheduled with teachers when syllabi can be checked, trends outlined, and new developments described. This is an important part of keeping schools up-to-date.

Unemployment caused by technological change and industrial reorganization places a burden on society and weakens the productive capacity of the nation. Insofar as possible, retraining and reassignment of personnel who will be displaced by dramatic changes in economic enterprise should precede their displacement.

The role of trade unions. Trade unions regulate to a considerable degree the flow of new workers into a given craft. An oversupply of labor generates restrictions, and young workers who seek to enter apprenticeships are turned away. Two factors bear heavily upon the vocational preparation program at this point. On the one hand, there is the recognized right of the student to prepare for a vocation of his own choosing; but on the other hand, there are the hard facts of the demand for labor in a particular craft and the opportunities for employment. Cooperative agreements between vocational schools and trade unions keep the schools informed of job opportunities and limitations and at the same time lessen the number of graduates who have trained for the trades in which job opportunities do not exist.

An excellent example of such an agreement exists in Connecticut. Here craft unions have cooperated with the schools in developing work experiences for students in carpentry, sheet metal work, electrical work, air conditioning, plumbing, and bricklaying. Under the terms of this agreement, the young people in the trade schools build a number of houses each year.

The integrating role of the schools. A number of community agencies, service clubs, and institutions sponsor activities that have vocational education and guidance implications. The Boy Scouts of America, Junior Achievement, 4-H Clubs, the YMCA, and the YWCA are examples of organizations which offer exploratory experiences to young people who are seeking to find vocational niches. In church-sponsored group meetings young people discuss ways to earn a living. Future Farmers, Future Teachers, craft clubs, and junior science groups offer opportunities for young people who have made tentative choices to explore them in some depth. Rotary, Kiwanis, Lions, Altrusa, and business and professional women's clubs give special attention to vocational education.

Most communities are rich with resources that have potential for developing the capacities of young people. The school that isolates itself from these forces is not serving its students well. Live, vital community-school programs do not happen by chance. They exist only when community leaders, together with teachers and administrators, see the whole community with its agencies, its institutions, and all its social and physical attributes as a laboratory for teaching and learning. A distributive education program or any other school-work experience program does not function well unless it is actively supported by community leaders as well as teachers and other officials in the school.

In rural neighborhoods and communities, young people in former years became intimately acquainted with agriculture, with homemaking, and with small business operations in and around country towns through firsthand experiences. Through work on their fathers' farms, they developed skills for handling livestock, cultivating the soil, selecting seeds, planting, and harvesting. They came to know the feel of work and to accept a sense of responsibility, for neglect or failure could well have meant the suffering or even the death of a farm animal, loss of income, and perhaps hardship on the entire family.

Community life in recent years has become much more complicated in all of its facets and operations—particularly in large cities. Direct work experiences cannot be so easily secured as in the simpler rural setting. But the range of opportunities for work experiences and their implications for vocational development is many, many times greater in the larger urban community. These opportunities cannot, however, be used without planning, without organization, and without conscious effort on the part of leaders who must feel and accept some sense of responsibility for helping young people become acquainted with and oriented to the world of work.

PLACEMENT

How to effectively bridge the gap between completion of a secondary school program and direct entry into gainful employment is a problem that has not generally been well met. Most schools do much better in assisting their graduates to find their places in colleges and universities than they do in helping students who do not go on to college to find places in the world of work, even though the number of students who enter some field of employment directly from high school continues to be greater in most school districts than the number of young people continuing their education in institutions beyond the high school level.

The school cannot become a placement agency, but it can go much farther than it does in acquainting employment agencies and personnel offices in large industrial plants with the competencies and attributes of the young people who have spent three or four years working with teachers and administrators in the school system. Establishment of good working relationships between the school and industries and business establishments that employ young people coming directly out of high school is crucial in introducing young people into the world of work.

TEACHER PREPARATION

The first requirement of a vocational teacher is thorough knowledge of his craft. The five years of successful journeyman experience traditionally required of shop teachers is an excellent foundation. However, mastery of the skills of a trade is no guarantee that an individual can transmit such skills to young people. The ability to teach people how to do something without taking over and demonstrating is a rare one. The instructional team approach which combines the craftsmanship of the journeyman with the ability of the professionally trained teacher would undoubtedly improve vocational education in many schools.

Vocational education teachers need to be familiar with the changing nature of occupations, the rate of change, the effect of job status upon the worker and his family, and the psychological effect of repetitive operations. They especially need to know how to transmit the cultural overtones of occupational employment—whether it be in a great industrial plant, a communications center, the growing field of sales and services, or the construction trades—through the teaching process.

Obviously, the vocational teacher cannot be expected to have more than a general overview of the vast range of occupations in which people earn a living. However, through visits to industrial plants and commercial establishments, through summer work experiences, through educational television and radio, and through continuous contact with business and industrial leaders, the vocational teacher can increase his understanding of the world of work and be more helpful to young people in their efforts to relate their school experiences to gainful employment.

With rapid changes in employment opportunities and shifts in the demands for labor, vocational teachers must be continuously retrained; otherwise, they will become obsolete, and their obsolescence will be transmitted to young people. State departments of education, universities, local school systems, and wherever possible business and industrial enterprise must cooperate in providing work-study programs which will assist vocational education teachers in keeping up-to-date with occupational change, employment opportunities, and manpower needs in this country.

PRIORITIES

A panel of consultants, reporting to the President of the United States following a nationwide study of vocational education, emphasized that—

> Vocational education is not available in enough schools.
>
> Vocational education is not available to all who need it.
>
> Vocational education is not preparing for enough jobs.
>
> Technical training after high school is critically needed.[1]

In an advancing technology and a culture that is becoming more and more complex, more skilled craftsmen and highly skilled technicians in occupations requiring scientific knowledge are needed. Many

---

[1] Panel of Consultants on Vocational Education. *Education for a Changing World of Work*. Department of Health, Education, and Welfare, Office of Education, OE No. 80020. Washington, D.C.: Government Printing Office, 1962.

more technicians must be prepared for employment in business, in industry, in agriculture, and in the fields of health services and personal services. In recognition of this need, the people of this country through legislative and administrative action at national, state, and local community levels have placed a larger measure of responsibility on the schools for—

1. Equipping each individual with the knowledge and skills needed to get and hold a job and to make a worthwhile and personally satisfying contribution to society
2. Meeting the manpower needs of society
3. Aiding in solving the problems of unemployment
4. Raising standards of living for people whose family income is low because of limited earning capacities.

What is done well in the classrooms and the laboratories—or, in unfortunate circumstances, is left undone—affects the quality of personal and social life and in the long run determines in great measure the values by which people live, the things they cherish, and the ends they seek to achieve. Ignorance and low human aspiration not only lessen one's ability to earn and his chance to contribute something worthwhile to the community, but they lessen his freedom. The individual who does not have the competencies required for employment is not as free as one for whom a wide range of occupational opportunities is open.

The need is pressing for better and more appropriate educational opportunities for all young people. If economic enterprise is to remain strong and vigorous, if the productive capacities of industry are to continue to grow, and if the individual is to remain free to shape his life in a manner of his own choosing and to be master of his own destiny, *it is imperative that vocational education programs in all communities be improved and expanded to meet the demands of the times.*

IMPERATIVE

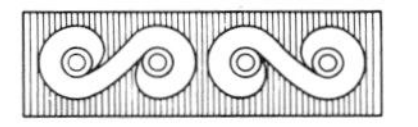

4 · TO DISCOVER AND NURTURE CREATIVE TALENT

Success stories depicting personal accomplishment and the amassing of material wealth without formal education, while still copy for enterprising feature writers in the Sunday editions of newspapers, are being reported with less frequency. The belief that creative talent will inevitably rise to the surface without being nurtured by carefully formulated educational programs may have had a semblance of validity in the past, but few would contend that individual goals or the pressing needs of contemporary society can be met in an unplanned, incidental way.

A society characterized by rapid change and unprecedented complexity cannot afford undeveloped or even underdeveloped human talent any more than it can afford waste in its diminishing reservoir of mineral deposits and other natural resources. In an earlier day, undeveloped human talent might have meant only unrealized individual ambitions kindled by native endowment. Now it may well mean failure to preserve a society and a way of life that free people are being called upon to defend around the globe. Failure to develop any human talent today not only is a personal tragedy but also may result in the inability of a people to cope with problems that if unresolved may lead to destruction and enslavement. With emergence of the atomic age, the development of space technology, the advance of scientific invention and inquiry, and the continuing ideological struggle for men's minds, *it is imperative that human talent of every kind, no matter where it is found, be developed to the maximum.*

The strength of a free society is dependent upon the full development of the potential of all its citizens. The development of individual skills, the acquisition of knowledge, and exacting endeavor may bring financial success, the acclaim of one's peers, and the realization of personal ambition; but there is more to human aspiration. Young people are attracted to the Peace Corps, teachers accept assignments in difficult schools, professional men serve in governmental posts at personal sacrifice, scientists spend long hours in the laboratory searching for a cancer cure, individuals protest injustice to others, not wholly because of a desire to meet pressing societal needs, but rather to satisfy the inescapable urgings of the human spirit to count for something. Failure to develop creative talent denies and limits opportunity to fulfill the best of human aspiration.

CENTRAL PURPOSE OF THE SCHOOL

No agency or institution in a free society is better able to discover and develop human talent than educational institutions. All children are required to attend a public or private school for a specified period of time. The school has as its central purpose the nurture of talent—encouraging and guiding pupils in the development of skills and acquisition of knowledge. Because public educational institutions are committed to serve all segments of society, an even greater responsibility devolves upon them than upon private institutions, for public institutions must discover talent that has not emerged, must be concerned with the unselected and the unheralded, must direct attention to a wide range of ability and to broad areas of interest.

It is recognized that students with creative potential are not always academically superior—that creative potential has a broad range of expression. Such talent may find expression in art, in music, or in social relationships. The television studio, the industrial arts shop, the gymnasium, and the student activity center are contributing to the development of creative talent just as are the library and the academic classroom. In New York City, and in some other school systems, special schools are provided to develop the special talents which are present in all student populations. The merit scholarship program and summer study opportunities sponsored by the National Science Foundation are further examples of efforts to develop the varied talents of youth. In many schools broad curricular programs permit exploration of a wide variety of interests. Activities provided by agencies outside the school supplement the schools' efforts.

It is literally true that from the "labs of Cal Tech to the lecture halls of MIT," in schools serving hamlets and urban centers all across America, all types of educational institutions are discovering the creative capacities of young people and are providing resources for their development. But unfortunately, far too many young people will never achieve the personal goals to which they might well aspire or contribute to society the discoveries and leadership of which they are capable, simply because the development of creative talent has not been considered the educational imperative today's world requires it to be.

John A., a graduate student in a Midwestern university, was being examined by a faculty committee as a preliminary step to approval of his candidacy for a doctor's degree. His major was mathematics. Completion of a master's degree with high marks indicated his potential as a doctoral student. In response to a question about a weakness in the broad field of literature that was apparent in his background, he reported that he came from a family of very limited financial means, that his father was illiterate, and that his mother had only a fifth-grade education. There were no reading materials in his home. His ability to read well was not acquired until he was in the ninth grade and a concerned business education teacher who recognized potential talent in an unlettered boy provided learning experiences for him after school and during the last period of the day when other boys were playing basketball. As a result of that teacher's concern and the legacy of a system of public education, not only is this lad well on the way toward his goal of an advanced degree in a critical field but an older brother has been encouraged to attain a master's degree and two sisters are in college. The fortuitous combination of a concerned teacher and a persevering lad susceptible to direction and encouragement combined to produce, not one scholar, but four individuals whose creative talents will bring satisfaction to themselves and contributions to society that otherwise would not have been possible.

Business enterprise, scientific research, military defense, teaching, governmental service, industry—every facet of the culture requires talented individuals who possess knowledge, skills, and imagination. One of the imperatives of education is to develop such talent. How shall this be done? What levels of education have primary responsibility for such development? What resources are needed? These questions require attention if this imperative is to be met.

DISCOVERY OF KNOWLEDGE

Emphasis on the discovery of knowledge, as contrasted with the memorization of facts discovered by others, characterizes the revolution in education. New approaches to learning in mathematics and science have been instituted in elementary and secondary schools across the land. Flexible scheduling to individualize instruction in order to facilitate the learning of the most able as well as the retarded has been instituted in many secondary schools. Colleges have developed honors programs, and many grant advanced credit to those with appropriate learning experiences. Enriched summer programs as extensions of the regular academic year are not unusual. Thus schools are attempting to vitalize learning, to extend learning horizons, and to develop the variety of abilities which a combination of nature and nurture can produce. The problem of meeting the needs of the intellectually competent, the creative, and the gifted, whose talents are and will be in such great demand, must have high priority for educators and those who administer educational programs.

Discovering the latent, undeveloped talent all children possess to some degree and providing opportunities for its nurture would be a demanding task even if enrollments were stable and the school's efforts were reinforced and abetted by the home and other community agencies. The fact that most schools are confronted by mounting enrollments and an increasing number of children who receive little encouragement or direction from the home adds to the difficulty. The school is faced with the dilemma of individualizing its efforts, a necessary task if creative expression is to be fostered, while more and more children are served.

Individualized instruction focusing upon the individual child is an essential ingredient of any program that consciously seeks to discover and develop the creative talents of children. This is true in part because creativeness has a unique quality about it. It differs in amount and kind. Furthermore, the optimum conditions for the development of creative skills and interests differ for each child depending upon environment, personality structure, and what some investigations of learning refer to as "distinctive cognitive style." Crutchfield, in his exploration of creative thinking, emphasizes the importance of individualizing instruction:

> It is increasingly recognized that to make the instructional process optimal account must be taken of the specific background, capabilities and distinctive cognitive style of the given individual. In order that any bit of instructional information—no matter how small—be properly understood and mastered by the individual, he

> must be enabled to assimilate it relevantly to his own cognitive structure, to transform it according to his own preferred and distinctive cognitive style, in such a way as to "make it his own." This requires individualized instruction that is geared to the distinctive attributes, needs and cognitions of the particular person.[1]

Individualizing the instructional program in the school is based upon the premise that there is a uniqueness about every child that requires specialized treatment if full development is to be achieved. This premise has implications for school organization, staffing policies, physical facilities, curricular and cocurricular programs, and resource utilization.

THE GIFTED

If schools are to meet their obligation in furthering the development of those with unusual talent, they must first of all identify those types of giftedness to which attention must be directed.

The gifted have been defined as those persons whose performance in any line of socially useful endeavor is consistently superior. Getzels and Jackson have directed attention to four areas of giftedness: intelligence, psychological adjustment, creativity, and morality.[2] Who can deny the importance of the full development of individuals who possess these desirable attributes and others to a superior degree? *It is imperative that the schools direct attention to the superior student in whatever area of superiority his undeveloped talent may exist, not only because each student is entitled to the assistance of the school, but because society profits from such development.* Equality of educational opportunity means educational opportunity appropriate to the needs and capacities of each child, the bright as well as the dull, the creative as well as the less imaginative, the child destined for a leadership role as well as the child who is destined to be a follower. The intelligence quotient is but one measure of superiority, present or potential: there is giftedness of many kinds in the spectrum of personal attributes.

Developing the talents of the gifted means a kind of education which is different not only in terms of the nature of the educational experience provided but also in the length of time formal schooling

---

[1] Crutchfield, Richard S. "Instructing the Individual in Creative Thinking." Address given at the Conference on New Approaches to Individualizing Instruction, Educational Testing Service, Princeton, N.J., May 11, 1965. pp. 1-2.

[2] Getzels, Jacob W., and Jackson, Philip W. "Educating for Creativity." *The Revolution in the Schools.* (Edited by Ronald Gross and Judith Murphy.) New York: Harcourt, Brace and World, 1964. p. 174.

shall be made available. Thus college and university attendance must be assured for all who can profit therefrom.

UNDEVELOPED TALENT

Included in the more than half of today's secondary school graduates who do not enter college are many whose talents will never be fully developed. These are youth who stop short of the formal preparation that would make it possible for them to assume significant and necessary leadership roles in society. An additional 10 or 15 percent who are potentially able to perform satisfactorily at the college level withdraw from school before receiving even the high school diploma. Erosion of talent also occurs during college: half of those who enter fail to graduate.

A further concern is the inclination of many unusually able young women to terminate formal education earlier than is desirable and to avoid entering many areas of vocational endeavor where they have aptitude but not the will to break with tradition.

DIVERSIFIED OPPORTUNITIES

The necessity for developing creative talent places heavy responsibility upon the public school and its administrator. To meet this responsibility, increasing numbers of youth must be encouraged and opportunity must be provided for them to continue their formal education at the post high school level. For some this means vocational schools where special skills, usually of a manual nature, can be learned. For some it means enrollment in terminal, technical programs in community colleges. For some it means enrollment in colleges and universities where educational programs can be pursued that culminate in the baccalaureate degree. For some it means enrollment in universities and participation in research for advanced degrees.

If the school is to discover the creative talents of all children and youth and provide appropriate programs for developing these talents, it is imperative that—

> Classes in elementary schools be small enough to permit the teacher and those who aid her to discover latent talent and provide nurture for it.
>
> Varied programs, particularly at the secondary school level, be provided to permit discovery and exploration of a variety of interests and abilities.

Special attention be given to the discovery of talent in children deprived of the kind of cultural environment that fosters its emergence.

A functioning program of guidance and counseling begin in the elementary school and focus upon the identification and measurement of potential abilities and the assessment of barriers that hinder the full development of such abilities.

To make these and other kinds of educational opportunities equally available to all, it is imperative that—

Appropriate compensatory experiences be provided for those children whose cultural inheritance is not likely to foster the emergence of desirable talent.

Economic assistance be made available to those who require it to permit, insofar as is practical, the full development of talent.

There be further expansion of technical schools, colleges, and universities in order that all who can profit from higher education can be served.

The development and nurture of creative and imaginative minds is not a simple task. Resources needed are in short supply in most institutions. Conscious and systematic effort to develop creativeness in children is largely an unexplored field. Instruction in creative thinking has received the attention of many research workers, including Crutchfield and his associates. Their research has been motivated by the belief that

> Virtually *every* child—regardless of level of intelligence, school achievement, and socio-economic background—needs and can substantially benefit from explicit training in creative thinking, that there is, in short, an enormous gap between his usual performance on creative thinking tasks and the performance he is really capable of.[3]

It seems logical to assume that other types of creative endeavor need more than just incidental attention. While it may well be that research has not provided practitioners with all of the essential dimensions of creativity and ways it may be nurtured, reason and empirical evidence suggest certain desirable practices and the character of optimum conditions for creative expression.

First of all the climate both in and outside the school must encourage original thinking, inventiveness, and the full exploration of ideas. Identification of the good student as an "egghead" or a "bookworm" does not promote such development. Physical prowess

---

[3] Crutchfield, *op. cit.*, p. 4.

brings public acclaim often at the expense of other forms of excellence. The climate within the school should be characterized by—

Unmistakable concern about each child's development.

Positive encouragement to explore interests and express feelings and attitudes in any acceptable way.

Freedom to differ, to pursue untried paths of inquiry.

Reward and commendation for the unique and unexpected—for achievement beyond normal expectations.

Availability of resources to support exploration of a variety of interests.

Opportunity for sharing the pursuit of special interests with peers.

Development of an inquiring mind, not just a filled mind, is a worthy goal in kindergarten as well as at the graduate level in the university—a worthy goal for all children but particularly for those who have unusual capacity for original thought and creative endeavor. Fortunately, new programs in mathematics and science beginning at the elementary level foster such development. The teaching of communications skills and the social studies is receiving similar attention. However, the memorization of facts and their regurgitation at examination time still characterizes much instruction at all levels.

Teachers frequently value most highly the student who conforms to their expectations, who avoids tangential excursions into unassigned areas, who accepts and does not question their judgment and that of other "authorities." The bright student with the high IQ is the prize student. That creative capacity may not so express itself has not occurred to many teachers. Perhaps most greatly needed are teachers with inquiring minds who can join students in forays in search of answers and solutions to perplexing problems. Thus teacher-preparing institutions have a significant responsibility.

A primary conditioning factor which contributes in a major way to the climate referred to above is thus the teacher and other school personnel. If creativity is to be fostered, such individuals must themselves—

Demonstrate creativity in work with children, in the selection and preparation of learning materials, in devising effective teaching methods and procedures, in exploring ways to improve effectiveness, and in developing ways to foster the flowering of creative expression.

Be comfortable with children who know more than they about some things and be able to place themselves in learning roles with the children as together they pursue interests.

Know how to create an atmosphere where there is the right balance between individual permissiveness for individual fulfillment and group restraint.

Recognize even a faint spark of unique effort and fan it into a glowing ember of self-expression.

It is imperative that the teacher's efforts to foster the optimum development of each child's talents be supported by school board policy, administrative leadership, curricular materials that emphasize self-discovery rather than rote memorization, and physical facilities that are functional but at the same time are themselves examples of creative expression.

Inflexible schedules, rigid curricular requirements, and narrowly conceived criteria for evaluating pupil progress will seriously limit, if not prevent, individual study and exploration essential in developing a wide range of interests and talents. It is essential that the program be organized in a manner that releases rather than inhibits the creative capacities of teachers as well as pupils. The program must be supported by extensive resource centers, adequately equipped libraries, and studios to which students have ready access. The program should provide seminars which permit students to test hypotheses and to match their wits with others of like ability under the direction of a skilled and imaginative teacher or discussion group leader and in which opportunities are provided to contribute new thoughts and new ideas, to weigh conflicting evidence, to organize factual materials and attempt to distill the true meanings from them, and to form generalizations.

Discovery and nurture of creative talent in the school do not just happen. It depends upon how the school interprets its purpose, what resources it makes available to achieve this purpose, and how the educational program is fashioned. Central, however, to the fulfillment of this purpose is the school administrator—his own creativeness and imagination, his ability to accept change as a product of creative endeavor, and his concept of the school he administers as an institution for discovering and nurturing the creativeness inherent to some degree in every child.

IMPERATIVE

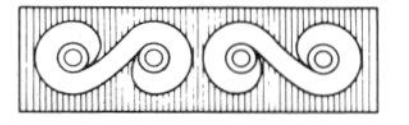

5 · TO STRENGTHEN THE MORAL FABRIC OF SOCIETY

Newspaper editors, writers, columnists, radio broadcasters, religious leaders, law enforcement officials, and educators are week after week and month after month calling attention to the deterioration of the moral fabric of society. There is an underlying thread in the expression of this concern suggesting that people of this age are innately ornerier and meaner than people were in former years. This inference can be disregarded, for human nature over the years changes only slowly. People are born with about the same characteristics now as in earlier times, but the culture around them in contemporary society leads to new behavior patterns, shifts in social controls, and situations in which new standards of moral behavior arise.

Deep-seated cultural values that have served generations of people as guides to social behavior are taking on new shades of meaning. Customs change with the times so that behavior patterns which were frowned upon and held to be offensive a few decades ago are now accepted as commonplace and actions that once seemed to have no moral significance now impair the rights and well-being of great numbers of people.

NEW APPLICATIONS

Fundamental values which undergird the American way of life, which have guided the actions of people for centuries, which have provided individuals with a sense of security in a wide range of circumstances, and which collectively in some pattern of relationships constitute the working philosophy of individuals in all walks of life, are being put to a severe test in this era of rapid technological change, social adjustment, and population expansion. What is of most importance to the school is that the points at which these values are being most severely tested seem to be most visible where the application of these values affects children and youth. Young people in colleges and universities and in the secondary schools must somehow be led to see with more clarity the relationship of the common good to the interest of the individual; the importance of productive work and individual initiative; the necessity for a sense of order among all things and all facets of the culture; the roles of basic institutions of society such as the home, the church, the school, and voluntary organizations; and the true significance in the American way of life of private property and economic enterprise.

Somehow young people, as well as their elders, must be led to see more clearly the perplexing issues that are emerging in relation to the whole civil rights movement and how these issues are related to the basic tenets of democracy, to the highest ideals of society, and to the rights and privileges of individuals. They must be led to see more clearly the material aspects of the culture as distinguished from its deep and abiding spiritual values.

CONFLICTING FORCES

People everywhere are confronted with conflicting forces. The concept of rugged individualism developed in an agrarian society is now being put to a severe test where individual voice and action tend to be submerged in organizations, giant industrial enterprises, and groups of many kinds. The concept of the town meeting as a form of democratic action cannot be readily applied in great cities. Many forces in the culture push people toward conformity. Rural-oriented values clash with the values that are predominant in an urban culture. Values and behavior patterns that are highly important in a congested city may not have been so pronounced in the isolated rural neighborhood where space for living was in abundance. Applications of values conflict at the ideological level.

Fromm, in discussing man's inner struggle to see the true meaning of life and to establish goals, comments:

> Man can choose only between two possibilities: to regress or to move forward. He can either return to an archaic, pathogenic solu-

> tion, or he can progress toward, and develop, his humanity. . . . Only the thoroughly "evil" and the thoroughly "good" no longer have a choice. Almost everybody can regress to the archaic orientation, or progress to the full progressive unfolding of his personality. . . . The problem of freedom versus determinism is really one of conflict of inclinations and their respective intensities . . . . One might generalize by saying that one of the reasons why most people fail in their lives is precisely because they are not aware of the point when they are still free to act according to reason, and because they are aware of the choice only at the point when it is too late for them to make a decision. . . . The longer we continue to make the wrong decisions, the more our heart hardens; the more often we make the right decision, the more our heart softens—or better perhaps, becomes alive.[1]

With culture changing so rapidly, people are searching for stability and sureness.

> Nowadays men everywhere seek to know where they stand, where they may be going, and what—if anything—they can do about the present as history and the future as responsibility. Such questions as these no one can answer once and for all. Every period provides its own answers. But just now, for us, there is a difficulty. We are now at the ending of an epoch, and we have got to work out our own answers.[2]

CHANGING CIRCUMSTANCES

The life about an individual, unless he has unusual strength of character, tends to shape his thoughts and actions. This is particularly true for children and youth. What happens to the values and behavior patterns of children when—

The family moves from a country lane or a small village to an apartment in a congested center of a large city?

The size of the school which they attend increases from 50 or 100 pupils to 2,000 or 3,000 pupils?

Most of the skills for living they have acquired in a rural neighborhood are of but little or no value to them or even may be a handicap?

The future well-being of the country as a whole and their individual well-being seems to rest in the manipulation of substances in a laboratory rather than deep and abiding spiritual concepts?

---

[1] Fromm, Erich. *The Heart of Man.* New York: Harper and Row, 1964. pp. 119-35.

[2] Mills, C. Wright. *The Sociological Imagination.* New York: Oxford University Press, 1959. p. 165.

The importance of group participation and team effort seems to take priority over individual action and initiative?

Their future depends in such great measure on their standing in class or the scores they make on a particular test?

They learn through improved skills in reading and communication that unfair employment practices, discrimination in housing, and measures to prevent citizens from voting are often condoned by distinguished leaders of society and are in conformity with established customs and mores?

Education has rarely been confronted with so many demands and with so many alternatives. What appeared to be the solid verities and certainties of the past are being vigorously questioned or have been supplanted by new knowledge and insight. As scientists, research workers, and philosophers probe the depths of old verities, there are fewer absolutes. Human relationships, institutions, value systems, and philosophies are in a state of flux. At the same time, this nation is cast in the new role of guardian of the heritage of human freedom. As Norman Cousins has so persuasively said, "Earlier generations have had the power merely to affect history; ours is the power to expunge it. . . . We have managed somehow to unhinge the permanent. Everything that has occurred in history until now has suddenly acquired interim status. . . . Our time has become a grand concourse for all the great causes and experiences of the race.[3]

The culture of this country and, indeed, of many countries of the world is shifting from the agrarian and mercantile civilization of former times to an industrial and technological civilization today and an automated and cybernetic civilization tomorrow. Some elements of the rich heritage from the past are on trial. Some that are obsolete will be discarded. Others which exploit men and make their lives brutish and sometimes short will be abandoned and forgotten. Still others—priceless ones—which constitute the best of civilization must be preserved. To save these is a major task of the times. To fail to comprehend the scope of the task is blindness. To assume that the task can be achieved by education alone is foolhardy.

Infinitely more complex industrial systems, rapid shifts in concepts of morality, many-splendored communications systems, dramatic increments of new knowledge, and other powerful and persuasive forces make peace, work, liberty, and equality vastly more important today than ever before. It is on these basic cultural foundations that a truly good life and a civilization must rest.

---

[3] Cousins, Norman. "Think of a Man: An Editorial." *Saturday Review* 39:9; August 4, 1956.

FOUNDATIONS OF ETHICS

The true worth of a civilization is found in its values, in its beliefs, in its feelings, in its preferences, in its aesthetic judgments, in its standards, in its measures of success, and in its commitments. "Whether he knows it or not," Mills contends, "the line-up of a man's problems—how he states them and what priority he assigns to each—rests upon methods, theories, and values." [4]

Writing in similar vein, Krutch says, "The most stupendous of [man's] inventions was not the wheel, or the wedge, or the lever, but the values by which he has lived . . . in the future as in the past, what becomes of him will depend less on what machines he invents or what governments are imposed upon him than on what values he creates." [5]

The cluster of values that lie at the heart of American civilization and determine in great measure the purposes and activities of people were not born anew with the early settlements along the Atlantic seaboard during the period of colonization. They are deeply rooted in the philosophy of the ancient Greeks; in the Judeo-Christian ethic; in the law and order of the Roman Empire; in the principles enunciated in the Magna Charta; in the establishment of parliamentary government; in the religious faith exemplified by St. Thomas Aquinas, Martin Luther, and John Calvin; and in the philosophy of Hobbes and Locke, who emphasized the dignity and importance of the individual.

Beliefs and commitments that have undergirded American life since the very beginning were brought to this country by the stern Puritan fathers; by the proud Cavaliers; by the patient and self-sacrificing Catholic missionaries; by fur traders, explorers, and swash-buckling adventurers who chafed at restraints and reached for new freedoms that seemed to lie just beyond the horizon. They were enriched and given new shades of meaning by the Dutch, the Swedes, the Norwegians, the Germans, the French, the Jews, and the Italians—by the waves of immigrants who came to this new country year after year until it grew from a small collection of frontier settlements into a mighty nation. Each newcomer brought with him hopes and aspirations, concepts of what is right and wrong, and something from his own culture that was assimilated into a total complex which has been referred to as "the American way of life."

---

[4] Mills, C. Wright, *op. cit.,* p. 128.

[5] From *The Measure of Man,* copyright, 1953, 1954 by Joseph Wood Krutch, reprinted by permission of the publishers, The Bobbs-Merrill Company, Inc. p. 172.

Deep down underneath this complex is a core of values that has given it character and purpose.

CHANGING VALUES

This core of values has not been static. Through three centuries of American history values have been emerging. They have been subjected to free and open debate. They have been tested along the Western frontier, in the quiet life of rural neighborhoods, and in the tumult of great cities; they have been on trial in the growth and expansion of industrial enterprise, in the interplay of voluntary organizations, and in the arena of political action; and they have been held up for penetrating analysis through mass media of communication.

Values change but slowly, yet they are always in the making. Each generation tests the values it has inherited against new and fresh circumstances. Yet values linger on and at times exert powerful influences on the behavior of people long after the circumstances to which they are most applicable have passed into oblivion.

Values are feelings, beliefs, and commitments distilled from human experience that may or may not be articulately expressed. They are influenced by knowledge, by environmental circumstances, and by the relationships of people to each other. They are often expressed in music, in art, in literature, in the character of institutions, and in the form and function of government. They are evident in the attitudes of people toward their homes, their families, the property they own, the occupations they seek, and the issues before them at any given time. Values are passed on from one generation to another in song, in legend, in legal statutes, in codes of ethics, and through the schools. They come to the forefront in religion, in politics, in courts of law, in social relationships, in opportunities for employment, in property ownership, in the modes of behavior predominant in community life, and in sense of personal responsibility for one's self and his fellowman.

THE AMERICAN ETHIC

The ethic of American life is based in great measure upon individual worth and dignity, initiative, freedom of choice, equality of opportunity, competitive spirit, respect for the rights of others, personal responsibility, and government by consent of the governed. These deep and abiding principles of the American ethic are not mere abstractions turned to only in times of stress or kept aloof from the rough and tumble of daily life for academic consideration. They take on meaning as they are applied in the commonplace, everyday actions of all people in their homes, on the streets, in neighborhood and community life, at their work, and at their places of recreation; they are guides to decision and action at the ballot box, in courts of law, and in employment practices; they are in evidence among children and youth on the school playground, in the classroom, in the back alleys, and at the corner malt shop; and they penetrate the quiet recesses of the student's innermost thoughts when he is pondering alternative courses of action or contemplating right and wrong.

At every level of human behavior, principles of ethical conduct and concepts of moral behavior quietly exert their influences. It is the capacity to choose, to sort one's experiences, to set proximate and ultimate goals, and to devise ways to achieve them that lifts human behavior to its highest level. It is through the discrimination of values and choices that one separates the good from the evil.

Human action may be divided into three great realms. The first is the realm where actions are controlled by laws which must be obeyed. The second is the realm where people commonly enjoy freedom of choice. The third realm is that large domain where neither rules, positive laws, nor freedom of choice prevails. This is the area of human behavior that is governed by ethical standards and inner sanctions. The course of action or the position taken on issues is determined by the individual. In a word, he becomes the enforcer of the standards which prevail.

Obedience in the realm of the unenforceable applies to those actions which the individual feels he should take, although he is not compelled to take them. It extends beyond free choice, for there is an inner compulsion, not wholly unrelated to duty as it is commonly understood, that exerts a strong influence on courses of action. This great principle of obedience to the unenforceable is strong in the hearts of most people. It is that inner force which causes youth and adults alike to put forth a little greater effort than is absolutely required, to shun the questionable, and to give voluntary support to what seem to be worthy causes.

Modern legislation tends to diminish the area of action which is governed by inner sanctions. The real greatness of a nation, the true strength of its civilization, however, will in the final analysis be the extent to which individuals can be counted upon to discipline themselves to obey inner sanctions and to be governed by self-imposed law.

The alternatives are clear: either inner sanctions to control actions are developed in the minds of people or controls are legislated and enforced by coercive measures. It is the development of these inner sanctions which so largely shape the character and personality of young people that so persistently challenges the schools. Effective problem solving aids in developing values because values are not abstract traits that stand apart from experience. Values are derived from human action, rather than imposed from without; they emerge where decisions of moral consequence must be made.

DEVELOPING ETHICAL CONCEPTS

There is good reason for contending that participation in the school as a community will have greater influence upon the pupil's values and judgments than the study of subject matter. School life is, in a very real sense, the child's life. The school is a complex of relationships. The administration, the beauty or lack of beauty in the school property, the orchestra, the schedule of classes, student government, the sports program, the halls, the library, the assembly, discipline, evaluation, encouragement and restraint, opportunity and lack of opportunity—all influence values. The child is enmeshed in a web of relationships where principles of right and wrong are continuously being applied. The school is the lengthened shadow not only of the administrators and teachers but of the custodians and clerks as well. It is in this community aspect of the school that the values, attitudes, and philosophy of nonteaching personnel shine through. What is called school spirit often takes its shape here. It is here that values are caught and taught. A friendly, wholesome school climate is indispensable.

The curriculum too is rich in value potential. In science, the student learns of suspended judgment and openmindedness and of respect for facts and a disciplined intelligence. He senses a relationship to the great laws of nature as he begins to comprehend the order of the universe, the vastness of space, and the infinitude of time. History portrays the rich heritage from ancestors and acquaints the student with issues and ideas and with the ideals which man has sought. Through the social studies he gains an appreciation of the democratic way of life, the worth of people, the rights of others, academic freedom, and the right to differ. Through literature and the fine arts he becomes conversant with human adventure, hopes, and aspirations and the problems with which man has wrestled throughout the ages.

Concepts of good sportsmanship, fair play, and respect for others; the importance of team effort; and the value of physical well-being are cultivated in many young people through sports and other extracurricular activities. Through the athletic program young people learn cooperation, courtesy, personal and group loyalty, and a whole galaxy of traits that affect their character and determine in no small degree their ethical and moral standards.

ENVIRONMENTAL INFLUENCE

The influence of environment on the attitudes and behavior patterns of young people is being reflected in school plants. During the past decade there have been marked changes in school buildings in nearly every community and neighborhood in the country. They have changed from heavy, massive structures with an awesome institutional look to informal, easy, fluid structures that seem friendly and inviting. Many builders seem to have caught the true spirit of childhood and youth and have transmitted it into form and structure. The upward surge for freedom that permeates every aspect of the culture has been recognized and brought into a material form of expression in outstanding new school buildings. These buildings mirror what goes on from day to day inside them.

Inside there are such innovations as individual study carrels, places in which a student can sit down alone to think and study on his own; small seminar rooms, in which groups of students can get together to work as a group on some project of concern to them that is related to their program of studies; snack bars, which encourage groups of students to come together, when they are free and unrestrained, to exchange ideas and to confer with each other briefly and informally; reading alcoves off the main floor of the library, where students can sit down uninterrupted to feel the deep satisfactions that come from sharing the experiences of a favorite author; and social courts which provide opportunities for students to mingle together during periods before and after school or during intermissions. Classroom furniture is mobile and can be arranged in different forms. Shops and laboratories give students opportunity to work independently, and large window spaces looking out on wooded and grassy areas provide visual relief from the shut-in feeling that comes to young children whose vigorous physical and emotional energy is bubbling at the fever pitch for release.

These structures indicate that teachers and administrators are putting more confidence in children and youth. They are more willing to trust them on their own, to help them develop a sense of freedom by living it and by learning to shape the standards that will guide their future action through living in a rich environment rather than one that is barren and meager. These buildings clearly show that teachers and administrators are fully aware that value patterns are being developed, that standards are being set, and that concepts of freedom and responsibility are being formed as children and youth live and work together in these buildings.

PINEY WOODS

Piney Woods School is located on a little rise of ground among the pines just south of Jackson, Mississippi. Here can be found one of the most striking illustrations in this entire country of how educational opportunity has brought to thousands of people a greater sense of freedom, personal worth, and commitment to high purposes than they otherwise would have had.

It was fifty years ago that Laurence Jones, a graduate of an Iowa university, without friends, without money, without acquaintance in the locality—without almost everything essential for establishing a school except a vision and commitment to a high purpose—began teaching the first student at the Piney Woods School. The classroom where this instruction took place was an abandoned sheep shed on a plot of land that had been deeded to an old Negro servant by the man for whom he worked, and the student was a little Negro child from an illiterate sharecropper's home. From this almost impossible beginning, and overcoming seemingly insurmountable obstacles, Dr. Jones persisted until now he has developed one of the best-known schools in the entire country.

As one approaches this institution over a winding road through a grove of pines, he suddenly comes upon a little knoll where there is a cluster of ten or twenty modest buildings. There are dormitories, classroom buildings, administrative offices, shops, laboratories, dairy barns, granaries, a butcher shop, a refrigerator plant, and a brick kiln. Amidst this cluster of buildings there is an attractive pool of fresh water with the surrounding land beautifully landscaped. Here and there are benches in the shadows of the trees where students can pause for conversation and study. Every building of this school has been constructed by the students. Every brick that is used in a structure has been made by the students. And the architectural design and the layouts for the entire campus have been done by the students.

Dr. Jones has patiently and determinedly pursued this long-range program of building this institution to serve people who were ignorant, who were underprivileged, who had little hope for the future, and who had no real sense of what freedom meant. He firmly believed that he could give them a sense of importance and bring their potential into fruition by giving them opportunities to learn the skills of the workman—to become artists, musicians, blacksmiths, dairymen, carpenters, painters, nurses, journalists, and teachers. The doors of this institution are open to anyone who wants to come and who is willing to work and to study.

Over the years, thousands of people whose lives would otherwise have been barren, bitter, and suppressed have had opportunities opened to them for rich and rewarding service and have felt a sense of freedom that in ignorance they never would have known. There are no bounds of freedom and responsibility prescribed by trade or occupation. The man who has thoroughly mastered the occupational skills in the field in which he works, who has perfected them to the degree that he gets satisfaction from his work and feels success in his accomplishment—be he bricklayer, house painter, meatcutter, or member of a learned profession—has drunk deeply from the cup of freedom and keenly feels his sense of responsibility.

It is the harshness of the situation and the desolate circumstances in which Dr. Jones worked that make his accomplishment stand out so clearly. What he has done for these underprivileged people has been done again and again in literally thousands of neighborhoods and communities for people in every part of the land—those who are less fortunate as well as those who are more affluent and self-reliant. This has been one of the great purposes and one of the great accomplishments of the institution of public education. Because of nearness to this institution and familiarity with it, one is prone to overlook what it has done to make men free.

FREEDOM AND RESPONSIBILITY

If there is one value that stands out preeminently in the American ethic it is the passion for freedom. Citizens in the community, teachers in the school, pupils in the classroom want almost above everything else to decide for themselves what they will do, where they will live, how they will use their talents and material wealth, whether they be great or small, and want to be masters of their own destiny. As Justice Brandeis put it, American people cherish "the right to be let alone." Such independence is a purpose and an ideal deeply rooted in national tradition. A large measure of the responsibility for clothing this ideal of freedom with meaning has been assigned to the public schools. Over and over again, administrators and teachers have asked themselves in the quiet of their studies, "How can the school best help a generation of young people to know the true meaning of freedom, to feel and know its true proportions in the day-to-day activities of the world about them, and to accept the full responsibilities that freedom of choice, freedom of decision, and freedom of action carry?"

This cherished characteristic in the behavior of people, this ideal of American democracy, is not something that is inherited, not something that can be legislated into being, and not something that can be dictated by a stern father or imposed by a tough superintendent. Freedom is not merely the absence of restraint. Freedom is a balance between the rugged disciplines and the harsh realities of life and the carefree spirit of a freckle-faced, barefoot boy with a fishing pole beside a lazy stream on a summer afternoon. It is a balance between firm commitment to a purpose or an ideal and the spontaneity of an untrammeled mind. It is a balance between the order and conformity imposed by society and the creative spirit that moves beyond the commonplace. Freedom is tough, it is independent, and it is self-reliant. Freedom is strength rather than weakness. It is the spark of genius that resides in every man. It is the basis for that creative individualism which has enabled the people of this land to meet challenge after challenge in every walk of life. It is the very essence of democracy.

Knowledge—reason—understanding—whatever it is called—has been the greatest moving force in developing high ethical standards. The Greeks in the fourth and fifth centuries before Christ demonstrated what mankind can achieve through the exercise of human intelligence and will. They trusted reason almost as the Hebrews trusted the Creator. In this Golden Age of Greece, which scholars have referred to as the Age of Humanism, the individual became the focal point of the cultural universe.

This cultural concept borrowed in great measure from the Greeks is deeply imbedded in the American ethic. It is the basis for self-government; the commitment to universal education; and the high priority given to creativity, research, and scientific inquiry. Forces operating in private and public life join in clothing the individual with dignity and respect, keeping him free to make full use of his talents in a manner of his own choosing, cultivating the inquiring mind, and nurturing the urge of people of all ages to know, to understand, and to question anything and everything. This is not only the spirit of personal freedom manifested by college and university faculty members in their persistent efforts to maintain academic freedom; it is also the insistence of leaders in the field of mass media for freedom of the press, the high public regard for free economic enterprise, the jealousy with which public control of education is guarded, the dissent of minority groups, and the chafing of college and high school students against the restraints of society. Herein lies the spark of creative genius—troublesome as it may be at times—that has led to social and cultural inventions and discoveries that have made life richer, better, and more satisfying for people everywhere. Self-determination is a criterion of growth. Society in the process of civilization expresses itself and moves forward through the actions of individuals who comprise it.

SELF-DISCIPLINE

He who lives life to the fullest and gets greatest satisfaction from it has a set of standards by which he tends to guide his own actions and behavior. Such standards are the basis for hopes and aspirations and for making decisions. Standards and ideals are hard taskmasters. Again and again they motivate young people and adults as well to put forth their best efforts—to do the best they can. All who have read Irving Stone's *The Agony and the Ecstasy* will recall that Michelangelo held to standards of perfection in his work that all of the adverse winds of deprivation, lack of recognition, family resentment, countless hours of backbreaking labor, and the changing whims of the political pressures of the times could not force him to abandon or compromise. In holding to them, he experienced an exhilarating sense of freedom richer and fuller than most people have known.

This is an unusual example, to be sure, but it is unusual only in degree. Everyone has some set of standards, but it is the quality of these standards and their relationship to one's fellows and to all society that count. *In attempts to strengthen the moral fabric of society, it is imperative that the schools help people to raise their standards and to learn how to live by and with them.* One may inquire, "How are such individual standards set?" No one really knows for sure—not even the individual himself—but experienced teachers and administrators through long years of working with people have discovered some leads.

Standards are the products of values. Values develop in individuals through the lives they lead. The better the life, the better the values.

If children are to develop and to hold high standards in their classroom work and in their relationships with those with whom they associate in every sphere of human conduct and behavior, they must be given opportunity to know what high standards are. All too often destitution denies an individual the chance to become somebody of true worth to himself and to the world.

OVERCOMING ADVERSITY

While there are great accomplishments in this country to which people can justly point with pride, leaders in responsible positions are tormented by the knowledge that thousands of children and youth are growing up in unsightly and unhealthy conditions in the congested sections of large cities as their parents strive to get a foothold in a culture that is strange and fearsome to them. The rate of high school dropout is but one index of the seriousness of the problem; delinquency, resentment against common controls that must be preserved in society, lack of self-discipline and self-confidence, and irresponsibility are others.

Choices are made on the basis of experience and unique purposes. Everyone has a background of experiences upon which his perception is based. He cannot clearly see that which he has had no preparation to see. Montaigne aptly wrote almost four centuries ago, "I have read a hundred things in Livy that another has not, or not taken notice of at least; and Plutarch has read a hundred more there than ever I could find. . . ." [6] One can see no further into a generalization than his knowledge of its details extends.

The individual is responsive to his environment. When the environment is foreboding, distasteful, and fearsome, he throws a psychological screen around himself and withdraws into it for self-protection. Children in the classroom, on the playground, in the neighborhood around their homes, and even in their homes and adults at their places of work or at social gatherings withdraw into psychological shells that shut them off almost completely from the world about them. Such shells become barriers that are difficult to penetrate, and the individual becomes a prisoner in a structure of his own creation. There is perhaps no greater limitation to individual freedom, to an inquiring mind, to self-development, than these intangible barriers which teachers and administrators meet and with which they must deal in some manner day after day.

---

[6] Montaigne, Michel de. "Of the Education of Children." *Great Books of the Western World.* Chicago: Encyclopaedia Britannica, 1952. Vol. 25, p. 68.

A sense of injustice often starts the process of building these psychological barriers and withdrawing into a shell. Feelings of injustice breed disrespect. The germs of disrespect are subtly planted in the minds of people, particularly children, by distorted values, frustrations, and feelings of inadequacy. These germs of disrespect, once implanted in a budding personality, are difficult to ferret out and to exterminate.

BUILDING SELF-CONFIDENCE

The child who is free and spontaneous, who is eager and receptive, who is forever seeking opportunities, who wants to try his hand at everything that comes along, who has a healthy curiosity, who is reaching out and up for a thousand different things—this child thinks well of himself, thinks well of others, and sees his identity with others. Such children look outward rather than inward. They feel themselves to be a part of a world in movement. Such people—children and adults alike—know the importance and the value of mistakes. Those who move forward to meet new challenges must know that mistakes may be made. If they are too fearful of them, they will not venture into unexplored territory and will refrain from attempting to do that which has not been safely done before.

It is perhaps at this point that responsibility must be related most clearly to freedom of action. The consequences of mistakes must never be too costly or freedom defeats itself and dire consequences may come to the individual and to all of those with whom he is associated. This is the delicate balance that parents and teachers and school administrators must maintain as they give constructive directions to the actions of those who look to them with confidence for guidance.

The person who is free is well informed. There is nothing more effective in releasing the human spirit from the bondage of superstition, apprehensions, and fear than knowledge and understanding. And there is nothing that builds in people the power to resist the forces which would dwarf their personalities, blemish their characters, instill in them low standards of ethical conduct, and deny them freedom more than knowledge and understanding.

No other institution has done as much to add to the sacred dignity of the individual as the public school. Every community and almost every neighborhood has a public school. It has served everybody. It reaches nearly everyone in a vital way. Billie Davis, the daughter of a migrant farm worker who followed the crops from state to state, found one open door in every community; that was the schoolhouse door.[7]

CULTURAL IMPACT

As teachers and pupils work together in the classrooms, they cannot be insensitive to overtones of the cultural problems and issues that come to the forefront in homes, in shops and factories, in columns of newspapers, in radio and television broadcasts, in casual conversations on the street corners, and in village council chambers. Here the questions of freedom and responsibility, of ethical standards, of independent action and human rights, of democracy and all that it holds for individual dignity come to the forefront in discussion of the broad problems that are before the country at the moment. There are overtones of uneasiness in this discussion about unemployment; increasing productivity; cooperation between labor and management; equal opportunities for employment, for education, for housing, and for the exercise of voting privileges; the morality of society; and relationships to other nations of the world. American ideals of freedom, self-government, and human dignity are placed in perspective against the backdrop of events in Vietnam, in the Dominican Republic, and in Latin America. These broad issues are vigorously debated between liberals and conservatives, between rural and urban dwellers, and between youth and their elders.

The real problem—to all Americans, but to the schools in particular—is that of dealing with these cultural developments in a way that will add to the dignity, freedom, moral stamina, and well-being of people rather than detract from them. The basic concepts of democracy sustained a youthful nation of people and served them well in developing a great and powerful country. Can these principles serve people equally well or better in dealing with a new series of challenging problems that a free people have created? How do the schools contribute most to instilling deep in the heart and mind of every student the sense of moral responsibility, the necessity for integrity, and the commitment to high ideals needed in this hour?

Teachers and administrators may get a lead from Tennyson. In "Ulysses," he said, "I am a part of all that I have met."[8] The language he speaks, the customs he accepts, the values he cherishes are all

---

[7] Davis, Billie. "I Believe in Our Public Schools." *Building Americans in the Schools.* Official Report of the American Association of School Administrators. Washington, D.C.: the Association, 1954. p. 138.

[8] Tennyson, Alfred. "Ulysses." *Victorian Poetry.* (Edited by E. K. Brown.) New York: Ronald Press Co., 1942. p. 27.

derived from his experiences. Mind, like body, flows in this stream of life. And one never quite recovers from any past experience, nor does one regain any earlier self.

How can the moral fabric of society be strengthened? How can students be taught the true meaning of freedom and responsibility? There is, of course, no one body of content, no cluster of experience, no tried and true procedure that will accomplish this end, but it may be helpful to teachers and administrators—indeed, to everyone—to call attention to a few possibilities.

> Let students be concerned with that which makes men free—not that all knowledge does not in some measure serve this end—beginning with that which directly and at the moment effects this purpose, be it a circumstance on the playground, a situation in the management of the school, or some incident in literature or history within their range of comprehension.
>
> Let an honest curiosity be cultivated in all students. Let them be inquisitive about everything about them and explore everything that is singular and rare. See that no restraining bounds in books or in subjects are imposed; and if there be eminent people, momentous events, or notable places in the school neighborhood, make them a part of their program of studies.
>
> Let them be curious in their search for reasons why this or that happened or a particular procedure was followed, but let them be seasoned to submit to truth whenever they have found it.
>
> Let them thoroughly sift through everything they read or each parcel of information that comes to their attention and seek more than one authority for substantiation of a fact or truth. An individual with a free and open mind knows full well that an assertion made by even an eminent man or woman is not necessarily true.
>
> Let them put whatever they have learned into a hundred different forms to see if they rightly comprehend it and have made it their very own.
>
> Let them put every lesson they have learned into practice whenever and wherever possible so that they learn at an early age the subtle art of transposing learning into living.
>
> Let them have their turns in discussion and discourse, parry with ideas, learn to discern, learn to discriminate and to choose, taste strange new fruits of learning, and try their wings while they can be guided.

Let them laugh and play and strive to excel their companions in ability and vigor, for the youthful spirit that is bridled and curbed and that does not have a chance to try and prove its strength is soon dull and stagnant—more fitted for subjugation than for probing into new domains.

Let them avoid vain and childish pretensions to being more accomplished than they really are.

Let them discover and acknowledge their errors and misconceptions wherever they exist, knowing that as such shortcomings are fully recognized by themselves, new measures of strength and stature and new dimensions of freedom are added to their lives.

Let them drink deeply of the satisfactions that come from work well done; let them know that work is not a curse.

Let them develop a sense of freedom and responsibility by living it, by helping to shape the standards that will guide their present and future actions.

Let them know that he who acts unjustly not only wrongs himself but harms others.[9]

---

[9] Indebtedness to Montaigne's essay, "Of the Education of Children," is acknowledged:

Montaigne, Michel de. "Of the Education of Children." *Great Books of the Western World.* Chicago: Encyclopaedia Britannica, 1952. Vol. 25, pp. 62-80.

IMPERATIVE

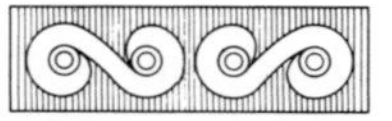

6 · TO DEAL CONSTRUCTIVELY WITH PSYCHOLOGICAL TENSIONS

This is an anxious age. The symptoms of the times are reflected in the uneasiness and restlessness of a growing proportion of the population. People everywhere are caught in the increasing pressures of a changing society.

Transition brings pressures. Though often subtle and unobserved, these changes are widespread and relentless. They uproot the lives of millions of families, confronting them with job loss, extended unemployment, change of vocation, and migration to urban communities where they are caught up in a web of unfamiliar, complex, and confusing social circumstances.

Among even the more fortunate families whose employment and status are secure, the confusing temper of the times often creates feelings of fear, insecurity, and anxiety. These growing tensions affect all facets of society. They affect school board policy, as is evidenced by the struggle over de facto segregation. They affect the work of the teacher in the classroom, the behavior patterns of children on the playground, and the action of teachers individually and collectively. They affect business enterprise, church congregations, and legislative assemblies. When permitted to develop unchecked, sustained tensions have serious, damaging effects on the personalities of people and on their effectiveness as learners, workers, and citizens.

These psychological tensions are highly contagious; they are transmitted within the family group and readily infect children. They affect learning and personality growth and play a significant role in the child's intellectual development as well as his emotional stability.

THE SCHOOL AS FACILITATOR OF GROWTH

One of the primary cultural goals of society is to help children grow into mature, self-confident, fully functioning citizens who are able to meet effectively the demands of life even amidst conflicts and tensions. Many social forces contribute to growing up; among them are the home, the community, religious institutions, recreation, and the school. The school is a major facilitating agent in helping the child grow toward self-actualization and social adequacy.

In its unique role as a facilitator, the school must utilize much of the influence of other forces and must be perceptive of their effects on the child's development. Their influence on the child's mental health is deep and critical and may be either for good or for evil.

EMOTIONAL PATTERNS

By the time the child reaches kindergarten or first grade, influences from his earlier years have already had a persisting impact on his emotional patterns, his language facility, and his whole personality. A large proportion of first-grade children who have lived in fortunate circumstances are already functioning adequately and fully at their six-year-old maturity level. Thousands of others who have been less fortunate are already psychological cripples. They are stifled by fears and ridden by feelings of insecurity or aggressive hostility, and their emotional and intellectual growth is seriously handicapped. Between these two extremes—the adequately functioning child on the one hand and the psychological cripple on the other—fall millions of other children with varying degrees of psychological conflicts and tensions, ranging from mild emotions to strong emotional conflicts that cripple growth.

SOURCE OF TENSION AND CONFLICTS

What brings about this psychological crippling—insecurity, anxiety, tension, and resentment—that so many children bring ready-made to school? This crippling is not necessarily the product of specific external circumstances or material conditions. It is internal, emotionalized, and subjective. It is not physical, nor is it necessarily rational.

Tensions and anxieties are psychological; they are born out of frustration and conflict that arise from the individual's thwarted needs. They emerge when the individual faces a situation that blocks the drive to fulfill his basic needs and is unable or not permitted to respond adequately enough to remove the block. When the blockage and the resulting tensions persist for prolonged periods, the personality is affected. Kelley puts it bluntly:

> We get that way in the same way that a physical cripple does—by the lives we lead.
>
> The newborn babe has enormous potential for health, but this health has to be built out of his experience with others. It has to be achieved, and it has to be achieved in relationship to others. The health potential then lies strictly in the quality of the people around him, since the infant, for many years to come, has, himself, no control over whom he will associate with.[1]

Mental health is dependent upon experience. A child may be psychologically crippled or develop a normal, healthy personality, depending upon the nature of his experiences as he lives and associates with people in his home, the neighborhood, or the school. If Kelley's assumption is valid—and he has the full weight of the mental hygiene group on his side—then parents, teachers, and administrators who live closely with the child in his growing-up years should strive to understand and be sensitive to the way the child's self-concept is achieved. For these key persons are working on the growing edge of the child's personality.

The human personality, healthy or unhealthy, is a whole lifetime in the making. It is not at any time—and never can be—a static entity; it can never be finally established. It is always *in process,* always emergent, always *a becoming.* The self—that inner core of the person that constitutes his real, unique identity—is thus constantly forming and re-forming out of its strivings to fulfill its own basic needs as it perceives them.

BEGINNINGS OF SELF-PERCEPTION—CONSCIOUSNESS OF SELF

Because of this continuum of striving to fulfill its needs, the child's *self* inevitably becomes involved with perceiving itself as it becomes more conscious of its own successes and failures and evaluates its own adequacy in meeting the demands of everyday living. Almost

[1] Kelley, Earl C. "The Fully Functioning Self." *Perceiving, Behaving, Becoming.* 1962 Yearbook of the Association for Supervision and Curriculum Development. Washington, D.C.: the Association, a department of the National Education Association, 1962. p. 11.

from birth, the child's concept of his inner self begins to evolve—the self-concept, the "real me." Very early he begins to see the self as generally all right, competent, adequate for the usual demands of everyday living; or he begins to feel the self to be lacking, inadequate, insufficient for whatever life is giving out. Much behavior is motivated by the individual's need to enhance his self-concept and to protect it from threats of various kinds.

"Many people in the world today," as Kelley points out, "suffer from inadequate concepts of self, which naturally lead to mistaken notions of others." [2] He elaborates:

> We see evidence of this all around us. We see people ridden by unreasonable fears. The fearful person looks at his self and sees that it is not sufficient to meet what he fears. Middle-aged graduate students are afraid to stick their necks out. They are afraid to write; they suffer from stage fright. The question uppermost in their minds is, "What will people think?" Their selves are veritable skeletons in their closets, and if one has a skeleton in his closet, it is best not to do anything except to keep quiet. Any move may reveal it. So they try to sit tight so that they may not be revealed to others. This is a great loss to others—to mankind—for new paths are forbidding and exploration is fraught with terrors.
>
> An inadequate concept of self, so common in our culture, is crippling to the individual. Our psychological selves may become crippled in much the same way as our physical selves may be crippled by disease or by an accident. They are the same, in effect, because each limits what we can do. When we see ourselves as inadequate, we lose our "can-ness." There becomes less and less that we can do.[3]

Prescott, summarizing experimental and clinical studies, concludes:

> . . . that *people carry ideas about themselves* that are powerful factors in shaping their levels of aspiration, ways of defending themselves from loss of self-respect, and, indeed, choice of behavior patterns in many situations.[4]

Prescott goes on to point out that the child's perceptions of self and the world strongly influence the way he acts in relation to the world.

> If he perceives the world as loving and valuing him and consequently as supporting, comfortable, and nurturing, then he will trust the world and be unafraid in it. He will expect to have his needs satisfied and to find pleasure in the process. In short, he will be psychologically secure.[5]

---

[2] *Ibid.*, p. 10.

[3] *Ibid.*, pp. 10-11.

[4] From *The Child in the Educative Process* by D. A. Prescott. Copyright © 1957. McGraw-Hill Book Company. Used by permission. p. 379.

[5] *Ibid.*, p. 385.

On the other hand, if his childhood experiences are accompanied by a high proportion of unpleasant feelings in the form of anxiety and insecurity, the same child may seek to avoid interaction with the world and resort to withdrawal. If he feels undue hostility from the world, he may assume a resentful, aggressive attitude toward people about him, particularly those in authority—teachers, parents, and police, for example.

Both the tendency toward withdrawal and the tendency toward aggressive hostility provide eloquent signals to teachers and parents that deep in the child's feelings all is not well with his world, nor with his self in relation to his world. These signals should be the more eloquent to teachers, for teachers are aware that the school *is* the child's world in large degree and that it constitutes one major part of his world of relationships.

CHILD'S SELF ON EXPOSURE

At school the child is constantly put to the test; he is called on to read, to write, to recite, and to perform in all manner of ways. To him there must appear to be no end to it. If all this were a private showing for his own viewing and self-evaluation, it would appear bad enough to him. But probably in no other of life's ongoing relations is the child's self and its adequacy or lack of it so relentlessly exposed to persons so close to him—persons whose judgment of his self and its adequacy are so important to him. These include his parents, his teachers, and especially his peers. And all this gets down inside the spirit of a sensitive child.

This is not too disturbing for the child who has been helped to develop the competencies that underlie school tasks and security and confidence in his inner self. It simply provides him with further opportunity to experience the excitement of success and reinforces thereby his positive self-perceptions. Out of such stuff grow further competence, confidence, and willingness to tackle other problems still more difficult and unfamiliar. Such success moves him along toward the goal of becoming an adequate, fully functioning person.

HARVEST OF FAILURE

The child whose experiences have been inconsistent or nonsupportive or who has not achieved the competencies needed to meet demands made on him—whether in everyday living, in school tasks, or in group cooperation—is quite different. For this child, the demands that face him often stretch his seemingly endless string of failures. Repeated failures defeat the school's and the home's overriding goal of helping the child move toward adequate functioning as a person. And the ill effects are not limited to his failure to acquire the specific learnings involved. Continuous defeat destroys even his *ability* to learn effectively.

One of the tragedies of the educational process is persistent "policies and practices that virtually condemn something like a third of our children to failure, dropout and a life of marginal existence." [6] If it is true that "we become what we practice," as the behavioral scientists insist, then in a setting where the individual is caused to practice continuing failure, he becomes to himself a failing person, developing tensions and an unhealthy self-concept which are emotionally harmful.

This holds special significance for deprived children. Teachers who work with deprived children report that they, more than others, are frustrated and more often become apathetic or rebellious in school when they cannot succeed at school tasks.[7] Erikson, in urging the importance of successful school experience, insists that the child's

> . . . danger, at this stage, lies in a sense of inadequacy and inferiority. If he despairs of his tools and skills or his status among his tool partners, his ego boundaries suffer, and he abandons hope for the ability to identify early with others.[8]

Much of the motivation for sound learning comes from the child's drive to enhance his self-concept through positive achievement and to protect it through avoiding failure. Where this is recognized by parents, teachers, and administrators, home demands and schoolwork are made flexible enough to meet the competence of the individual rather than geared to group averages.

EFFECTS OF MENTAL HEALTH ON LEARNING ABILITY

As already pointed out, healthy personality (a positive, adequate self-concept) is achieved through one's experiences with the people

[6] Melby, Ernest O. "Needed: A New Concept of Educational Administration." Address delivered at Southern Illinois University, as reported in *The Community School* (Board of Education Building, Flint, Michigan), July 1965. p. 1.

[7] Bloom, Benjamin S.; Davis, Allison; and Hess, Robert. *Compensatory Education for Cultural Deprivation.* New York: Holt, Rinehart and Winston, 1965. p. 47.

[8] Erikson, Erik H. *Childhood and Society.* New York: W. W. Norton & Co., 1950. p. 227.

among whom one lives. Since mental health and effective learning are definitely and reciprocally related, the teacher and parent need a clear concept of what constitutes the healthy individual in this sense. The healthy individual is confident and efficient in learning and problem solving, constructively productive, realistic in self-appraisal and in goal setting, able to accept and give esteem and love in interpersonal relations, and happily committed to significant personal goals.[9]

A clear perception of the unhealthy or maladjusted individual is perhaps as crucial for parents and teachers. Frandsen traces the emergence of emotional disturbances in learning through the following sequence:

> Children observe that *accomplishments* win them rewarding approval from their parents, teachers, and peers. Thus the achievement of competency becomes a cultural ideal and the basis for feelings of personal worth, esteem, and confidence. Failure to meet the standards of parents, teachers, and peers threatens the child with loss of esteem and love and leads to feelings of inferiority, guilt, and anxiety. As . . . modes of adjustment to threats (to the self) and to the accompanying anxiety, individuals learn such defenses as substitute gratifications, denial, repression, displaced hostility, self-punishment, regression, and avoidance of learning. Excessive dependence on these . . . account for the ineffective learning and problem solving of the maladjusted individual.[10]

Frandsen points out further that the psychological stress of frustration may sometimes impair the learning and thinking abilities of anyone, but that the anxious, maladjusted person is especially prone to such disturbances. Poor mental health can inhibit the basic process of learning.[11]

Thus it is seen that when the individual is caught up with psychological tensions, more than his emotions is involved. His intellectual abilities are impaired, his motivation level drops, and his will to keep trying is greatly diminished. As he attempts then to compensate by unacceptable behavior patterns to save his self-esteem, he calls down on himself greater disapproval or even rejection from parents, teachers, and peers. This drives him further to the wall, and his potential to perceive, to think, and to learn becomes progressively more impaired. Many a child considered dull, lazy, stubborn, or "no account" has simply been caught in this vicious cycle of maladjustment brought on by the psychological tensions produced in his unsuccessful attempts to meet the expectations of those about him.

---

[9] From *Educational Psychology* by A. N. Frandsen. Copyright © 1961. McGraw-Hill Book Company. Used by permission. pp. 205-40.

[10] *Ibid.*, p. 425.

[11] *Ibid.*, p. 424.

SUBJECT MATTER LEARNING AND PERSONALITY GROWTH

Up to this point, the child's personality development and emotional adjustment have been considered largely in the context of the child's concept of himself and of his relations with others. Another principal ingredient in his self-concept is his skill and competence as shown in his accomplishments. The fact has already been emphasized that success is an emotional tonic and failure a depressant. Learning is the heart of the school program—in large degree learning subject matter—for subject matter learning lies at the center of much of school experience. Helping the child *learn how to learn* can make a significant contribution to his self-concept and may often change his whole attitude toward those about him.

Tom's is a case in point. Though from a good home, Tom, for some reason, brought feelings of inadequacy to the first grade which began immediately to pervade his school experiences. He promptly developed confirmed reading problems. Tom's reading deficiency and his perceptions concerning it persisted through four years and brought him to loathe school and dislike anyone connected with its operation—even, to some degree, his parents, for they kept close to Tom and his school problem. Then, finally, he advanced to Miss Gordon's fifth grade. After four weeks with her, Tom remarked to his mother one evening, "You know, Mother, I've decided something about Miss Gordon. I think she *likes* to help boys learn to read." Tom's reading skills began to improve, and so did his feelings toward school, teachers, his parents, and himself. His new growth in reading skill was slow—as growth always is. But success in reading brought pride and confidence that gradually began to transfer to other parts of his schoolwork, and then to his personal and social relations with his associates both in and out of school.

As with Tom, improvement of basic learning skills almost invariably pays off in helping the troubled child. Its importance should not be underrated. Some insist that the high incidence of truancy and delinquency among children from disadvantaged communities may be rooted in the poor teaching sometimes found in schools due to overcrowding, poor facilities, frequent movement of families, and other factors that retard learning.

Mental hygienists emphasize the importance of helping insecure children learn how to learn in school. One says,

> If one wants to aid a child, it is not always necessary to give him a complete psychoanalysis. A teacher may give a child the affection he needs by helping him to learn. . . .

> When any youngster needs affection, the simplest way for teachers to administer it is not by honeyed words or sympathetic smiles, but by friendly assistance in learning. . . . For this reason, the skills of a good teacher who can help children find success in learning are as specialized as those of a psychiatrist. . . . Good teaching gives boys and girls a type of support which they see as meaning they are liked and which can be accepted by many youngsters who would be frightened by more direct affection.[12]

The effective teacher must have much more than personal warmth. In addition, he must have the professional competence essential to help pupils learn how to learn. Both are highly important, with each quality complementing the other in good teaching.

Helping the child to become a more competent learner meets many of his inherent basic needs and helps advance him toward maturity. It increases his feelings of adequacy and his self-respect. Competence in the things his school group admires brings respect from the group—the basis for increased feelings of belonging. In learning how to learn he gains security. Out of this comes confidence, for nothing succeeds like success. He has broken his old cycle of failing because he did not try and not trying because he failed.

The importance of school learnings is doubly significant in these times when the school is regarded by so many as the best hope for improving the lot of the maladjusted, the slow learner, and the disadvantaged. Fuller recognition of the role that learning plays in personality development may lead to adjustments in the instructional program that will help many emotionally upset children now regarded as beyond hope get started on the road toward self-improvement.

TENSIONS AND THE CHANGING VIEW OF INTELLIGENCE

Research in the behavioral sciences is revealing the effects of emotional tensions on intelligence. New insights are causing people to reject the conventional concept of intelligence as a fixed ability to learn—an ability that one is born with, that rigidly stands throughout life, an unchangeable ceiling that cannot be lifted. The research work of students of intelligence is leading them to see that intelligence

> . . . rather than being fixed by genetic factors at birth, emerges as it is nurtured. Each stage of development carries with it possibilities for the acquisition of new abilities, new ways of processing information. Unless each of these abilities is exercised as it emerges, it will

[12] Redl, Fritz, and Wattenberg, William W. *Mental Hygiene in Teaching*. New York: Harcourt, Brace and Co., 1959. pp. 206-207.

> not develop fully and it will contribute little if at all to the demands of the next stage.[13]

This view of intelligence has important implications. If learning ability (intelligence) is emergent, developmental, dependent on nurture, then the home, community, and school have major responsibility for providing a climate for nurturing it. Instead of writing off slow-learning individuals as dumbbells or misfits to be discarded, this new view insistently demands that they be perceived as persons whose growth potential has been undernurtured. The obvious next step is to provide a program that will compensate for deficiencies in their backgrounds.

This new perception holds that one's current intelligence is largely ability "to receive information through the sense organs and to process it." More than ever in American life, this focuses attention on the quality of the child's past experiences, on whether these experiences have helped him learn how to learn, and on how they have affected his personality. It also attaches prime importance to the effects of emotional maladjustment on the individual's ability to learn.

These new perceptions concerning the character of intelligence call for reappraisal of the uses currently made of intelligence tests. It may be accepted from empirical evidence that present intelligence tests do measure functional or operating capacity at a given point of development and that they are fair in this respect. But the belief that they can measure innate potential and fixed ability is being increasingly questioned. In the past this concept of tests frequently caused teachers to adopt a fatalistic view toward the child with learning difficulty and to reject him as genetically deficient, when the real source of his intellectual deficiency lay more probably either in an impoverished background that failed to nurture his intelligence potential or in a climate interlaced with psychological tensions that led to crippling maladjustments.

These new insights into intelligence do not eliminate the concept of individual differences. They recognize actual differences in the nervous systems of individuals that may give one child *potential* for a higher level of intellectual development than another. The significant facet of the new view is recognition that the potential for intellectual development of a high proportion of people is never nurtured into full realization.

---

[13] Almy, Millie. "New Views on Intellectual Development in Early Childhood Education." *Intellectual Development: Another Look.* Papers from the ASCD Eighth Curriculum Institute. Washington, D.C.: Association for Supervision and Curriculum Development, a department of the National Education Association, 1964. p. 13.

After summarizing the evidence for this view of intelligence as a potential that must be nourished into development, Deutsch challenges teachers and administrators:

> Examination of the literature yields no explanation or justification for any child with an intact brain, and who is not severely disturbed, not to learn all the basic scholastic skills. The failure of such children to learn is the failure of the schools to develop curricula consistent with the environmental experiences of the children and their subsequent initial abilities and disabilities.[14]

From this position, then, Deutsch proposes a rich nursery school program for all children, starting at three or four years of age, to provide the nurturing that is needed for optimum development of the intelligence potential, to prevent future disabilities, and to remedy current skill deficiencies.

THE SCHOOL AND NEED-FULFILLMENT

Inseparably related to this view of intelligence as *developed* potential is the role of the school as the nurturing agent. The foundation of public education derives much of its support from the thesis that associated living, properly organized and directed in the right spirit, adds to the quality of a person's life. Next to the home, the school is the most influential institution for fostering this process of associated living.

The child lives a large portion of his waking hours in constant interaction with teachers and peers in his school group. Since both mental health and personality are affected by one's experiences with other people, *it is imperative that the school's climate be favorable to emotional growth.* This school climate should nurture the healthy child's emotional development as well as meet the disturbed child's need for redirection of his emotional development. A favorable classroom climate nurtures positive health and avoids or compensates for crippling tensions. It is sensitive to the way children approach their fulfillment in both positive and negative ways.

A helpful frame of reference for planning and sustaining favorable classroom climate is found in Maslow's five categories of basic needs: physiological needs, safety needs, love needs, esteem needs, and the need for self-actualization.[15] These, he insists, are hierarchical in or-

---

[14] Deutsch, Martin. "Facilitating Development in the Pre-School Child: Social and Psychological Perspectives." *Merrill-Palmer Quarterly* 10: 258; July 1964.

[15] Maslow, A. H. "A Theory of Human Motivation." *Psychological Review* 50: 370-96; July 1943.

ganization. The fulfillment of any given category depends on the satisfaction of prior needs. This concept is based on the assumption that healthy individuals whose needs in the lower categories—physiological, safety, love—are satisfactorily met will strive continually for self-actualization. When, on the other hand, the individual's needs for love, esteem, and security are unmet, his energies are spent in anxious efforts to satisfy these needs in lower orders and thus are diverted from the pursuit of constructive goals.

The child cannot accept school goals or group responsibility as long as his energies are focused continuously, and probably unconsciously, on avoiding further loss of love and esteem. It is quite difficult, for instance, for an individual to have or to express love for another when for prolonged periods his own physiological needs are not being met. If he is continually hungry, tired, cold, and in rags, his organism is unconsciously more absorbed with this physiological level of his own needs than with his affectional relations with others. Unable, under these conditions, to give love in any considerable degree, he is also unable to accept it and thus often turns in hostility and rebellion against those around him. All this, in turn, diminishes his self-respect and self-esteem and further erodes his self-concept. His drive (hunger) to become a fully responsible person is constantly thwarted in advance by his feelings of unmet needs, step by step, as they arise on the respective lower levels. Self-actualization (the child's ability to operate according to his own motivations, standards, and values) is thus a difficult goal for the child unless his physiological, safety, love, and esteem needs, each in its turn, are being met within his day-to-day experiences.

In addition, the child's problem of satisfying a complex of needs, many of them in play concurrently, is further confounded by his own immaturity, inexperience, and the insecurity that comes from growing up. The school provides for many children the only experiences in their lives adequate to lead to healthy emotional adjustments.

THE RAW NEED VERSUS THE FEELING OF NEED

In dealing with these basic human needs, it is not enough to meet the raw need per se. The child's feeling about the need also must be satisfied in the process. One example, in the area of safety, will suffice here: Charles, in the first grade, became upset during swimming lessons because of his acute fear of the water. As the days went on, his emotional disturbance appeared progressively more severe, in spite of the fact that conditions had been established by the pool managers that guaranteed almost absolute safety in the pool. Because of the staff of competent lifeguards, it would have been virtually impossible for one to drown, even in a deliberate attempt. The point here is that the heart of the problem with Charles was that he *felt* insecure. This feeling of insecurity was as disturbing to his personality as real insecurity would have been.

In many situations in the home, in the school, and elsewhere, actual needs are met without recognition that it is the child's *feeling about* his needs that counts. It is not enough that he be secure from danger: he must feel secure. He may actually have the parent's or teacher's love and esteem. But this alone is not enough. They must express and communicate these feelings to him in such ways that down deep in his inner self he feels them to be true. Knowledge that the child's *feeling* of need must be satisfied as well as the need itself makes it essential that the teacher be intelligently perceptive as he directs and observes the interactions of pupils in the classroom. The teacher's sensitiveness to the child's feelings is invaluable in planning, directing, and evaluating activities for emotional growth.

THE SCHOOL PLANT

In a good school, the classroom itself, the school building, the grounds, and the whole environment are designed for comfort, beauty, convenience, and functional effectiveness. Each part of the building reflects a sensitiveness to maturation-level needs of the age-group that lives and works in it. The first-grade room is significantly different from the instructional spaces for fourth- or sixth-grade pupils in arrangement, design, equipment, scale, and furnishings. The same is true of all other areas of the building.

Good school architecture reflects awareness of the child's physiological needs for health, convenience, free physical activity, and comfort. In its design and appointments, the building shows sensitivity to the child's basic needs for a feeling of self-confidence and security. The size and design of the furniture and other equipment are appropriately scaled to the children's development level, and it can be easily and functionally manipulated by them.

In developing building plans, administrators sensitive to children's needs give prime attention to providing areas other than conventional classroom spaces. For even young children, there are spaces for library books, growing plants, science collections, and art displays, appropriately designed and equipped for the age level. There are spaces for creative play, for sitting, visiting, and relaxing. There are gardened areas rich in beauty where children learn though experience not only to enjoy beauty, but to respect and protect it. The auditorium and assembly rooms give live, firsthand experiences in the performing arts—orchestral, dramatic, and choral performances—all appropriate to the child's age level. Other parts of the building contain museum and laboratory facilities to further acquaint the child with the world in which he lives.

GROUP CLIMATE

Each classroom has its own emotional climate or atmosphere. One classroom may have a general atmosphere of acceptance, goodwill, tolerance, and belongingness. The atmosphere in another classroom, even in the same school, may be dominated by prejudice, cliques, rivalries, and rejection of those who are different. In the first group, teamwork comes easily; the inclination is to work together and to think of group members as helpers on the team. In the other classroom there are jealousy, suspicion, and antagonism; and in still another an indifferent, lethargic attitude of "What's the use?"

From a mental hygiene point of view, the quality of group atmosphere is critically important for every child, but particularly for one under tensions. To work in a climate heavy with threat, insecurity, disorder, or even laissez faire indifference puts the child with tensions under especially heavy pressure.

In attempting to characterize classroom situations, distinctions have sometimes been made between a teacher-centered classroom and a learner-centered classroom. The teacher is more dominant in the teacher-centered classroom, relying on directives, exhortations, and coercive measures to set the patterns of classroom behavior. In the learner-centered climate, the teacher's actions are more frequently reassuring, commending, clarifying, exploratory, and directed toward problem solving. The learner-centered classroom provides a climate of encouragement and support for the child with tensions.

NEWLY DESEGREGATED CLASSES

The importance of group climate is especially acute where wide differences exist in social or ethnic groups within the classroom. When population shifts and changes in school policies bring new ethnic groups into the school, tensions emerge because of the newness of the circumstance, preconceptions, prejudices, and lack of understanding. They are further compounded when racial groups are newly integrated. An emotionalized atmosphere may be created that is disastrous because of the tensions and conflicts it creates for the students in both the majority group and the minority. For the already insecure, anxious child, this can be highly destructive.

The basic problem is how to get children to live together without undue friction in such a classroom despite prejudices and stereotypes. The nub of the problem from the mental health viewpoint is to keep the school's prime objective of meeting the needs of individual students clearly in focus. This cannot be done unless the teacher is keenly sensitive to the feelings and attitudes of individual pupils and fully aware of points at which their security is threatened, their self-confidence weakened, or their desire for acceptance and esteem unmet. The ultimate goal of the teacher must be to help each child see other members of the group as individuals in their own right rather than as stereotypes.

Because high feelings often prevail in the community when integration is in process, both groups expect the teacher to take sides. This contingency must be met beforehand by a clear statement of what is expected in the behavior of children. Operational procedures must be firm, fair, and consistent with accepted standards of behavior. The teacher in such a classroom must view this whole problem with honest realism. He cannot develop a wholesome classroom atmosphere by pretending that prejudices do not exist among children or that they will go away if ignored. Frankly facing up to the realities and considering them forthrightly is the soundest approach to easing tensions and stilling uneasiness in both groups.

The experienced teacher knows full well that integration is not the sole cause of children's problems, that many of the anxieties that create tensions among children existed long before this issue came to the forefront. To place the blame for every difficulty that arises on this new problem is to add to its complexity. The classroom climate in a good school newly integrated strives to become a climate of "self-conscious search for an atmosphere of congeniality. . . . Every child present senses the respect for him, irrespective of his background or his color or his religion; he is recognized for the human promise that he is." [16]

Here is a major opportunity for the administrative leader. The superintendent and his staff and the school board do much to set the tone of realism and acceptance necessary for dealing with the many-headed problem. The attitudes of administrative leaders determine largely whether teachers can achieve a feeling of confidence,

---

[16] Russell, James E. *Change and Challenge in American Education.* Boston: Houghton Mifflin & Co., 1965. pp. 54-55.

security, and faith essential in approaching the problems inherent in this issue with full integrity.

TEACHER AS PART OF CLASSROOM CLIMATE

Somewhere in folklore is the legend that "when one looks at an object for a long time, one comes to look like the object." Superstition aside, empirical observation affirms that when faced day after day with a teacher who is irritated, anxious, and frustrated, the child soon becomes such himself. Conversely, when associated with a secure, patient, affectionate, generally well-adjusted teacher, the child himself begins to take on these qualities. In short, good mental health is contagious; poor mental health likewise is highly contagious; and the teacher is one principal carrier.

The well-adjusted teacher is free to become child-oriented and problem-oriented. As Peck and Mitchell put it:

> We say that he is "free" to be this way because he is not laboring under the burden of his own personal problems, which could sap his emotional strength and leave him little time or energy for anything else. He enjoys solving classroom problems because he has not been whipped by his own personal problems. He has patience because it has not been severely tried by his own personal exasperations. Such a teacher creates a desire for learning and an eagerness for life in the minds of his students because he himself feels this way about learning and life. And he communicates these feelings to his students.[17]

The teacher with tensions is likely to see a classroom problem as a personal threat and react to it out of his own frustration and insecurity. He may deal with a discipline problem in a personal, vindictive manner. His own feelings of insecurity are communicated to the pupil. Unhappily, among the maladjusted teachers in the classrooms today, a disproportionately high number are assigned to deprived communities, where need is greatest for emotionally stable teachers.

THE TEACHER'S OWN ADJUSTMENT DIFFICULTIES

It must be recognized that even under favorable conditions, teaching has some special psychological problems of its own. The realization that he is professionally obliged to put the student's welfare above his own interests and desires sometimes causes the teacher to develop

---

[17]Peck, Robert, and Mitchell, James V., Jr. *Mental Health.* What Research Says to the Teacher, No. 24. Prepared by the American Educational Research Association in cooperation with the Department of Classroom Teachers. Washington, D.C.: National Educational Association, February 1962. p. 24.

frustrations. He may be forced to restrain the spontaneous impulse to punish or to submerge his own feelings of prejudice. Quite often his assignment puts him in a community where the customs, habits, and values are so far removed from his own that it is difficult for him to reconcile the differences. This often tempts him to reject the community and its children.

The teacher may become disturbed with the slow pace of community improvements, change in values, and acceptance of new curriculum content and may become frustrated by the difficulty of easing the psychological conflicts that have such telling effects on the personalities of children. Community pressures may block the introduction of teaching practices which the teacher keenly feels should be introduced or may direct his efforts toward less worthy ends. Conflicts within the teaching staff may create disturbances that upset the teacher's sense of security and well-being and make him less able to assist children in dealing with their emotional problems.

In good school systems, the teacher himself, the whole teaching staff, and in particular the administrators forthrightly face the possibilities of such frustrations. Every discerning educator is aware of the destructive effects of teacher frustrations, especially for the psychologically upset child. To help teachers grow as persons, alert administrators seek to relieve pressures that bedevil teachers and create feelings of frustration. Evidence from both education and industry indicates that morale is higher when workers know administrators are aware of their needs and make efforts to meet them.

THE PRINCIPAL'S ROLE IN REDUCING EMOTIONAL CONFLICTS

Teachers expect the principal to handle difficult problems involving relations with parents, community leaders, and the central staff and unusual problems with students. When the principal serves effectively in this role, tensions among the faculty are diminished; but when he falters or fails to meet his responsibility, tensions spread among teachers and pupils, personality problems intensify, and the school's effectiveness is diminished.

The principal's attitudes and his manner of reacting to problems are highly contagious among the faculty and the student body. When he is understanding, confident, relaxed, and sensitive to the feelings of others, the whole faculty and student body reflect his sense of well-being. But if he is insecure, impulsive, or given to spontaneous criticism or seeks to place the blame for his own shortcomings on others, teachers are likely to work with children in the same spirit, and tensions multiply.

The principal's leadership is enhanced, and tensions and frustrations are reduced, when he understands enough about emotions and group interaction to keep everyone's attention focused clearly on the prime goal of the school—helping the child to learn effectively—and away from personalities. Redl and Wattenberg make the following suggestions for improving the principal's leadership role and maintaining a climate of staff relationships relatively free from disturbing tensions:

> *Keep routines to a minimum.* Unnecessary restrictions . . . raise the probability of tension.
> *Listen.* Much talk relieves the speaker's feelings.
> *Use democratic processes.* . . . Democratic . . . procedures reduce the harmful outcropping of aggression.
> *Respect established hierarchies.* . . . Many adults find it nerve-racking to try to serve two masters or to please two different people.
> *Back up teachers.* Nothing destroys morale faster than for a principal to fail the teachers when they expect his support.
> *Minimize the evils of cliques.*
> *Show equanimity when mistakes are made.* The less upset the principal acts when a teacher makes a mistake, the less anxiety will the teacher feel.
> *Establish friendly relations with the community.* By building good rapport with community leaders, a principal can reduce . . . pressures upon teachers.
> *Keep detail in its place.* . . . It is hard enough for a teacher truly to give priority to the needs of children.
> *Be flexible.* When new problems are met effectively in new ways . . . teachers feel more sure of themselves.
> *Give criticisms in private.* . . . a teacher's prestige with colleagues and students is very important.
> *Recognition of parental roles.* People who work with children may have more need than others to feel close to an authority figure.
> *Appreciate role as example-setter* . . . . if his emotional management of daily situations is wise, the wisdom will spread. If he remains cheerful under attack or when confronting problems, unafraid of admitting mistakes, and capable of dealing with juvenile misconduct without paling with alarm or throwing a tantrum, the same qualities are bolstered in the staff.[18]

These suggestions embody the most basic principles of mental hygiene. The effective school principal practices them consciously; he interprets them to his faculty; and by example and encouragement, he leads the faculty to understand, accept, and practice them in their own interstaff relations and teacher-pupil relations in the classroom. In this way, these principles of mental health become incorporated in all intraclass relations and thus pervade the climate of the class-

[18] Redl and Wattenberg, *op. cit.*, pp. 501-502.

room, the playground, and the school as a whole. Such a climate is a laboratory for sound personality growth.

INSERVICE EDUCATION FOR TEACHERS

Most teachers are conscientious, hardworking, and doing their best to help children overcome whatever maladjustments they bring to school and grow into healthy, well-adjusted persons. Whatever the school does to promote sound mental health in the near future will be done largely by teachers now in service. However, many of these teachers—probably most of them—have had but little professional preparation for dealing with mental health problems. Professionally minded and willing as they may be, they are handicapped in dealing with emotional adjustments—as much so as if they were teaching science without any training in that field. Consequently, teachers, particularly in neighborhoods and communities torn with tensions and emotions, need inservice programs that will help them meet and deal with these delicate but all-important psychological problems.

A growing number of teachers are becoming voluntarily involved in a great variety of inservice programs that lead to better understanding of the psychological problems that confront children. Growth in ability to understand and deal with mental health problems of children may come from provisions that permit teachers to work with security and confidence, opportunities for teachers to fulfill their own emotional needs, organized programs for the study of child growth and development, agencies to which extreme cases may be referred, and consultation services for teachers. These self-growth experiences may take many forms, such as teachers meetings, books, pamphlets, films, consultants, or formal courses.[19]

Experience has shown that in order to be effective, a program of inservice education must not only have the approval of the superintendent and his staff; it must have their complete involvement and commitment. Prescott, with a rich background in this field, contends that the understanding of and sincere belief in the value of the program on the part of the superintendent, supervisors, and principals is a really crucial factor:

> A program is unlikely to be very successful if it is merely authorized by the central administration, provided for in the budget, and then largely forgotten by the persons who run the school system. For child study is not a theoretical study but a way of acquiring insights

[19] Rankin, Paul T. "Fostering Teacher Growth." *Mental Health in Modern Education.* Fifty-Fourth Yearbook, Part II, National Society for the Study of Education. Chicago: University of Chicago Press, 1955. Chapter 15, pp. 354-74.

> that affect day-by-day decisions in the classroom and that lead to various kinds of adaptations in the operation of schools. It is important for administrators to share in these insights so that they can see the reasons for the changes that occur or are sought by participants . . . . administrators are busy people, carrying terrific responsibilities, and sometimes so preoccupied with other matters that they do not receive the necessary communications.[20]

Most teachers take advantage of these opportunities, when available, to increase their understandings and skills in the mental health field. They recognize more clearly that children *are* different; that behavior is *caused;* that parents and home background are the two best sources of information. Through these programs, teachers are able to recognize more clearly that much of a child's behavior is related to his efforts toward self-development and that such behavior becomes unsatisfactory when circumstances are not appropriate to his maturity level.

Reports clearly indicate that changes in insights, attitudes, and practices resulted in an improved emotional climate in classrooms and reduced strain and tension among both teachers and children and between teachers and parents.

ADMINISTRATORS PROVIDE THE LEADERSHIP

Many administrators are establishing effective programs to help teachers come to grips with emotional adjustment problems. They believe that programs in mental health are as significant to the well-being of children as arithmetic, science, and social studies. Some of these leaders insist that while substantial expenditures are made to improve programs in the languages, science, mathematics, and English, the country can ill afford to ignore the increasing problems of mental health in a world of increasing social pressures.

Somehow teachers must find the answers to three basic questions that thread through all their working relationships with children: (a) What occurs between teachers and children that is harmful to the learning, adjustment, and development of children? (b) What knowledge, skills, attitudes, and values relating to human development and behavior should a teacher have in order to work effectively in the classroom? (c) How can such understandings and skills be developed?[21] *It is imperative that these questions be satisfactorily answered and that these challenges be met.*

---

[20] Prescott, *op. cit.,* p. 480.

[21] American Council on Education, Commission on Teacher Education. *Helping Teachers Understand Children.* (Edited by Karl Bigelow.) Washington, D.C.: the Council, 1945. p. 454.

IMPERATIVE

7 · TO KEEP DEMOCRACY WORKING

If one were able to discern and to pull together the deep-seated desires of all people in this country, *keeping democracy working* would be high on the list of what people want. It was for the purpose of making democracy work that the public school was envisioned and established when the nation was in its infancy. It is in keeping with this purpose that schools have been supported and cherished until they have matured into the grandest design for universal education that the world has ever known.

Never before has democracy been of such vital significance in the lives of the American people—in the life of all America. Never before have so many people in different parts of the world been so deeply concerned about establishing democratic institutions. Never before has democracy faced so great and grave a challenge at home and abroad.

THE CHALLENGE

Thoughtful people in all walks of life now seriously ask whether or not this scheme of government and this way of life established in a simple agrarian society and sheltered by the barriers of great distance and great oceans can continue to flourish in a technological age when the barriers of isolation no longer exist and relationships with other nations of the world become more intimate and more complicated with each passing year. The common response to this awesome question is a resounding affirmative. But even the most casual observer clearly sees that democracy is being severely tested by great issues emerging at home and abroad. By its very nature—being of the people and by the people—anything less than the best efforts of all the people will lessen its chances for continued success.

But what is democracy? The dictionary tersely defines it as "government directly by the people collectively." In the words of those who framed the Constitution, democracy is "we the people." The author of the Declaration of Independence expressed one of its basic tenets in the phrase "all men are created equal." The democratic ideal was in the heart and mind of Lincoln when he urged his fellow countrymen to resolve "that this nation, under God, shall have a new birth of freedom and that government of the people, by the people, and for the people shall not perish from the earth." The Educational Policies Commission, in its historic statement in 1938, identified as basic concepts of democracy *the general welfare, civil liberty, the consent of the governed, the appeal to reason, and the pursuit of happiness.*[1]

Most people see democracy as a way of life that involves freedom to make choices about what one does, where he lives, and how he uses his earnings; the operation of institutions—the home, the church, and local, state, and federal government; the right of property ownership; social justice; the absence of caste and class barriers; equality of opportunity; and solution of common problems through the exercise of the free will of all the people.

But democracy is more than a heritage and privilege bought by the sacrifices of those gone before. It is a responsibility of every American and every freedom-loving person. Democracy is doing justice; it is respecting the rights of others; it is meeting one's obligations to himself and to his fellowman.

Rossiter says democracy is a "spirit which has pervaded the thoughts and directed the actions of governors and governed alike." It is a process "of arriving openly, through discussion and compromise, at decisions in keeping with the reasonable wishes of the majority, and then of pursuing these decisions with the fullest possible respect for the legitimate rights of the minority." [2]

The emphasis at every point is on *doing*. In words that will long remain as a guiding beacon for all Americans, John F. Kennedy, in

---

[1] National Education Association and American Association of School Administrators, Educational Policies Commission. *The Purposes of Education in American Democracy*. Washington, D.C.: the Commission, 1938. pp. 7-8.

[2] Rossiter, Clinton. "The Democratic Process." *Goals for Americans.* A Report of the President's Commission on National Goals. New York: American Assembly, Columbia University, 1960. pp. 61-62.

his inaugural address, said, "And so, my fellow Americans: ask not what your country can do for you—ask what you can do for your country."

In this crucial period of history when the eyes of the world are upon America, when the principles which undergird this way of life and the processes through which democracy operates are being weighed and tested by people everywhere, when the problems that confront democracy are becoming more complicated, and when the decisions that people are called upon to make at the ballot box are more difficult to understand and have greater consequences than ever before, responsibility for keeping democracy working and growing stronger rests especially heavy on the schools. If decisions that people make on common problems are based upon narrow prejudices, emotions, misconceptions, and information that is only partially true, the real spirit of democracy is weakened and the well-being of the nation is placed on shaky ground. But if the decisions made by people are based upon sound information, clear thinking, and the exercise of reason guided by commitment to high purposes, democracy will remain on a firm footing and become stronger.

ALL PEOPLE

Those who have spent their lives in education, who have faith in the power of education and a deep commitment to the high ideals of democracy, cannot accept the premise that only a small percentage of the total population is capable of acquiring the understanding necessary to participate intelligently in the solution of broad social problems. They cannot accept the premise that decisions on vital questions should be made by a select group of people and that only minor and inconsequential matters should be submitted for consideration and decision to the total population. They cannot accept the premise that the ingenuity of man has created a culture so complex that only a select few can fully participate in it. Firmly committed to the belief that every man should share in shaping his destiny, school people feel a great responsibility for developing in all people backgrounds of information essential for intelligent participation not only in government but in economic enterprise and in the total life of the community.

This responsibility is in essence the responsibility for teaching citizenship, but teaching citizenship under a set of circumstances more challenging and more trying than in former years—circumstances in which a great majority of the people have been brought together with relative abruptness in great urban centers; circumstances in which great numbers of people have organized into special interest groups and voluntary organizations; circumstances in which the basic principle of property rights comes into conflict with the principle of civil rights; circumstances in which questions of vital concern to an individual citizen—even though he may live in the most remote neighborhood of the country—may have their origin in distant lands; circumstances in which interdependence between one part of the country and another part of the country—between one segment of the economy and another segment of the economy—is far greater than in past years.

To help a generation of young people prepare as fully as possible for intelligent and effective participation in a democratic way of life under these circumstances is an overriding educational imperative. The grave question—indeed, the central question—that confronts all school people and all Americans is, "What can the schools do to keep democracy working?" Let no mistake be made—the America of tomorrow and the democracy upon which it will stand are surely being shaped in no small degree in the tens of thousands of schoolrooms where nearly one quarter of all the inhabitants of the land are becoming acquainted with their cultural heritage and with life about them and are being taught that democracy is for the average man the best form of government yet devised. This purpose of education was envisioned by Thomas Jefferson two centuries ago. It was never more vital to the well-being of the country than it is today.

It is imperative that the schools, to the greatest degree possible, give every child, youth, and adult as much education and as broad an education as his capacity will permit. There is no place in this educational program for prejudging the individual and deciding that because of his race, creed, or environment his potential is limited. To the extent that the school fails to provide an opportunity for every individual whom it touches and serves to develop his fullest potential; to prepare for a full personal life; and to acquire the skills and understanding essential for participating intelligently and effectively in government, in economic enterprise, and in the total life of the community and the nation, the school will have fallen short of its high purpose.

For everyone who has the ability, the way to a college education should be opened. For countless others who can qualify, the way must be opened to the community college.

In the past quarter century, because of scientific achievement, economic growth, and cultural advancement, the productivity of the average man has doubled. In that time, median educational attainment rose from grade school graduation to high school graduation.

The median educational attainment must rise to the level of junior college or other post-high school achievements by 1980 if democracy is to remain a leading form of government. This end is clearly evident in recent federal legislation in support of public education.

There must be special educational opportunities for the gifted, no matter in what areas their talents lie. Giftedness exists in some measure in a great many people and in greater measure in a few. But even if nature and circumstances make the possession of exceptional gifts the blessing of relatively few, a democratic society makes the opportunity to share in these gifts the privilege of all. Only as the search for and the development of the talented and potential leaders succeeds will the mastery of those forces which lie as yet beyond the cyclotron and man-made satellites be achieved.

There is also the great group of people who will not move on to college, on whom democracy's success—America's success—depends in such great measure. For each of them, there must be no less than completion of comprehensive high school or technical high school education. In spite of power-driven automated machines which relieve people of routine labor and backbreaking drudgery, the number of people gainfully employed in the labor force increases and there are unmet needs for technicians, skilled craftsmen, sales- and servicemen, farmers, and transportation workers in the enormous economic development ahead. Demographers predict that there will be 50 million more Americans in 1980 waiting to be served, fed, and satisfied and that the gross national product will rise to the nearly incredible total of $1.2 trillion.

But if democracy is to continue to work, another great group of Americans must be taught and trained and provided with job opportunities. The neighborhood or community that does not have some of these children is rare. They live in sparsely settled open country areas, in more heavily populated suburban communities, and in ghost lumber towns. But their number is greatest and they are most visible in the great cities. They are the newcomers who have had limited opportunities for intellectual, social, aesthetic, and physical development; the not so new residents who are oblivious to the opportunities surrounding them; and other residents of the city who have rejected educational opportunities because of insecurity, distorted values, lack of family encouragement, and limited aspirations. They are of every race and creed. They come to the city from the rural areas where automation has reduced the need for unskilled workers. They are the restless migrants searching for better jobs and better living conditions. They are the newly arrived immigrants from other lands. The children from these families have been called the "culturally deprived," "the educationally handicapped," "the dropouts," and "social dynamite." They are everywhere, but they are in and of the cities particularly. It has been estimated that in 1950 one pupil in every ten in the great city school systems was a deprived pupil; in 1960, one in every three; and it was predicted that by 1970, one of every two pupils in the great city school systems would be a deprived pupil.[3]

The teacher sees in the deprived student's response and condition inadequate communication skills; socially unacceptable behavior; indifference to responsibility; nonpurposeful activity; physical defects and poor health habits; retardation; poor attendance; high rate of failure; high dropout rate; low aspiration level; little kindergarten experience; negligible participation in cultural activities; and a potential which appears to exceed what test data suggest. Is this student's case hopeless? It must not be, if the city, democracy, and America are to remain strong. Environments can be improved, and children and young people can be helped to rise above their environments. Improvements will be made when the real educational needs of children coming into the schools from deprived circumstances have been clearly and fully identified and programs developed to meet these needs.

Elements of such programs that have been tried and proven to be successful in many school systems include prekindergarten education; kindergartens that develop habits, attitudes, and skills, including reading readiness and first steps in reading and arithmetic; remedial programs for older children to further develop and strengthen basic skills; teachers with sympathetic understanding of the backgrounds and problems of children from deprived circumstances; class size that will permit individualization of instruction; books, supplies, equipment, teaching devices, and specialized services realistically related to the cultural backgrounds and educational needs of these children; school-community coordinators who help parents become positively oriented toward education and the schools; full cooperation with governmental programs instituted and operated to reduce poverty and to improve education in all areas; adequate physical examinations with effective procedures for referrals leading to remediation of defects; adequate guidance at the elementary school level as well as at the secondary school level; and curriculum content that will help students come to a real understanding of the life about them, heighten their aspirations, and motivate them to achieve to their full capacities.

---

[3] Riessman, Frank. *The Culturally Deprived Child.* New York City: Harper and Row, 1962. p. 1.

When fully developed, the instructional program for these children will be a comprehensive community-school program that involves the home, churches, the neighborhood, business and industry, and the school all working together to provide an effective learning environment for them. It may include part-time work such as is provided under the Neighborhood Youth Corps program. It may include evening programs for older youth. It may include occupational placement and follow-up services. And it certainly will not overlook the importance of wholesome recreation. This will be an expensive program—a program that calls for greater expenditures of funds than have commonly been allocated to the schools in large city systems. But these costs must be met. Failure to provide an educational program that will help a generation of children to become effective citizens would be far more expensive than the cost of appropriate and adequate instruction.

The city is more than a center of industry, business, transportation, government, medical services, and cultural institutions. The strength, vitality, and greatness of a city is in its people—people who work, study, raise families, participate in community activities, and enjoy wholesome leisure. If a considerable number of people in a city are unemployed, discontented, restless, and in conflict with the orderly processes of community life, the strength of the city slowly dissipates. And if the city weakens, one can well ask, "What will happen to the suburbs, to metropolitan areas, to the whole country?" Democracy cannot fully function unless the full potential of citizens is developed and each is meeting his full responsibilities.

It is imperative that all schools have the best curriculums and use the best known teaching procedures. The combination of cultural forces emerging through rapid cultural change makes it imperative that school administrators and teachers seek new insights into the content of the curriculum and into the processes of teaching and learning. The vitality of the school program is dependent in great measure upon its sensitivity to the basic concerns of people. Whether one looks to the field of business administration, commerce, production of economic goods, social mobility, or social psychology, he discerns factors and forces that affect and shape people's lives and that determine how and to what extent they get along in the world. These forces are highly complicated, technical, and rapidly moving. They demand a higher degree of skill, alertness, understanding, and commitment than has been required of all the people in any previous period of history. To deeply imbed these understandings and commitments in the attitudes and actions of all people is a basic purpose of the school.

No curriculum, however well planned, can remain adequate for a considerable period of time unless it is constantly being revised to meet changing circumstances and conditions. Such revision must in great measure be done through and by the teachers. Teachers are close to pupils and know their potentialities, their hopes, and the problems that confront them. But to meet the responsibilities for curriculum planning and revision that will be placed upon them in ever-increasing degree, they must become more sensitive to society's needs and understand more fully the educational implications of the cultural forces that impinge upon the schools and upon the lives of people.

There can be no doubt that the schools are moving in the direction of new and better curriculums, better teaching methods and devices, and better student participation. Sensitive to the need for meeting new educational problems emerging in a rapidly changing culture, people through local, state, and federal government are initiating and sustaining special programs for handicapped children, for the potential dropout, and for the mature citizen whose occupation may have been disrupted by changes in job opportunities. Imaginative and creative teachers, supported by their school boards and the citizens of their communities, are initiating new methods of instruction, organizing new bodies of curricular content, and reaching out toward the forefront of cultural development. Here, without any attempt at a complete survey of innovations, attention is directed to a considerable number of forward-looking developments:

MATHEMATICS

All School Levels

Programed elementary mathematics, algebra, geometry, and calculus

Modern mathematics: sets, frames, modules

Elementary Schools

Beginning arithmetic in kindergarten

Greater Cleveland Mathematics Program

Cuisenaire rods, first year

Numeration systems, factors and exponents

Secondary Schools

The "discovery" method of teaching mathematics

School Mathematics Study Group (SMSG) materials

Electronic data processing practices

Computer mathematics, matrix algebra, symbolic logic

SCIENCE

All School Levels

Modern science laboratories, micro-projectors

Elementary Schools

University-connected programed learning experiments

Science courses beginning with grade 1

New AAAS science program as part of a national experiment

Secondary Schools

Demonstration kits for microbiology, biochemistry, radioactivity

Radiation measuring instruments

Enrichment in radiobiology, astronomy, advanced biology

Radioisotope distribution centers

Simulated space capsule projects

Physical Science Study Committee (PSSC) experiments

LANGUAGE

All School Levels

Reading clinic analysis services

Transparencies and overhead projectors for written English

Science Research Associates (SRA) reading laboratories

Elementary Schools

Linguistic approach to reading, grades 1-2

Trained volunteers in the reading program

Phonics "clinics" conducted by trained parents

Studies of rhythm in speech development

Secondary Schools

Linguistic approach to grammar, aided by TV

Speed reading, research, and critical reading

Great Books programs

Individual projects for underachievers

Foreign Languages

All School Levels

Modern audio-lingual method

Elementary Schools

TV French and Spanish, grades 1-6

Conversational French and Spanish

Secondary Schools

German, Italian, Russian, Hebrew, Chinese, Portuguese, and other languages

Electronic language laboratories

Electronic tapes in French and Spanish, grades 7-8

Audio-lingual-visual experimental French courses

Experiments with new tapes in patterns of language

Social Studies

All School Levels

Expanded use of museums, historical places, cultural centers, industrial plants, business offices, and communications centers

Living history through the use of the daily newspaper

Elementary Schools

Constructive citizenship programs in social studies

Increased emphasis on geography

SRA laboratory in reading maps and graphs

Secondary Schools

Visiting consultants in Asian affairs

Students and teacher participation in World Affairs Council activities

Classroom discussion on controversial issues

Student good grooming campaigns

Theory and Practice of Economics a required course

VOCATIONAL PREPARATION

Secondary Schools

Vocational guidance

Career conferences, forums, workshops with consultants

Home management, child development in home economics courses (39 percent of today's brides are under 20 years of age)

Graphic arts and electronics in expanded industrial arts courses

Tape-controlled machines in up-to-the-minute shops

Electronic shorthand laboratories, with choices of dictation speeds

Key punch operation as part of business data processing

Technical high school—thirteenth- and fourteenth-year courses: data processing, instrumentation automation, X-ray technology, medical technology, dental assistant training, and others

MUSIC AND THE ARTS

All School Levels

Organ instruction, with provision for practice

Visits to cultural centers, theaters, concerts during and after school and on Saturdays

Famous musicians, artists, actors on educational TV

Choral centers for choruses and solo voices: instrumental centers for orchestras, bands, and individual musicians operated after school hours

Elementary Schools

School resource files of parents with special talents

Visits by students from art colleges and museums

Secondary Schools

Electronic tapes as nuclei for music courses

Painting techniques shown by famous artists in school assemblies

Enrichment programs in public and private schools

Health and Safety

All School Levels

A comprehensive program of health instruction with selective and sequential development of health concepts at all grade levels, K to 12

Extension of the programs for safety on the streets, at school, in the home, and at work

School medical and health service programs with effective follow-ups

Elementary Schools

Planned health snacks for recess

Lunch programs

Mental health programs for underachieving students

Secondary Schools

Expanded athletic programs with a number of teams in each major sport

Handicapped Students (in addition to usual programs for the blind, deaf, crippled)

Elementary Schools

Classes for emotionally disturbed children

Music therapy for retarded-trainable pupils

Linguistic approach to reading for visually handicapped pupils

Classes for retarded-trainable pupils with special work in cooking, sewing, and use of tools

Secondary Schools

Expanded school-work programs for retarded-educable children: restaurant practice, hospital practice, library practice

Lowering the Dropout Rate

Secondary Schools

Special tutoring

Student volunteer tutoring programs

Specially designed college preparatory programs

After-school, in-school, evening-school, and Saturday programs

Evening home visitation programs

Occupational practice courses to help students adjust to the world of work (Students in these programs spend half of the day in class strengthening their knowledge in the fundamentals and learning how to hold a job and the responsibilities of the good citizen. During the other half of the day, they are in the shops learning simple occupations, usually of the service type.)

Business workshops to change attitudes and teach duplicating and typing

School-work programs in which students spend one half of the day in school and the other half at a job

Cooperative school-community programs to prevent dropouts

Human Relations

All School Levels

Teachers' guidebooks

Parent education programs

Action-research seminars for principals, teachers, parents

Elementary Schools

School-neighborhood projects designed to raise cultural levels

Father-son and mother-daughter nights

Faculty-parent shows

Preschool workshops for parents and children

Secondary Schools

Annual conferences on human relations

Youth institutes on human relations conducted in cooperation with community agencies

High school editors' conferences on human relations

New Approaches and Techniques

All School Levels

Educational television with programs produced by the school system using well-trained producers from its own staff and master teachers (The great value of this medium has been proven. It can be employed in the large group or class situation. It is a boon to the homebound child. Educational television is used for basic courses at all levels. It is used for enrichment programs; for bringing the expert from government, business, and industry to the student; for teaching cultural appreciation and art and music techniques; for stimulating health programs; and for inservice education of teachers.)

Elementary Schools

Educational improvement programs for deprived children: classes of fewer than thirty with a permanent teacher in every class, consultant services, school-community coordinators, and adequate supplies of books and modern equipment

Nursery or prekindergarten classes, particularly in deprived neighborhoods

Head Start programs

Hospital clinics and universities cooperating in studies of underachievers

Secondary Schools

Recordings through computer service

Speech improvement with tape recordings

University-connected projects for underachieving students

Adult Education

Adult retraining programs including those financed by funds made available through the Manpower Development and Training Act

English, Spanish, Italian, and other language programs in neighborhoods where needed

Parent-child nursery programs with weekly fathers' nights

Programed learning in reading, writing, and arithmetic for adults

---

Ideas for Tomorrow

Approved research centers for talented students

Digital computers for every senior high school

College-level biology and electronics courses in summer schools

Geography, anthropology, sociology, psychology, and history in a new organization of studies, K to 12

Fundamentals of business data processing in all comprehensive high schools

Group therapy for parents of handicapped children

Programs for preschool-age blind children

Extended tutorial programs

Expanded adult industrial programs

Counseling after school and at night in all areas

It is imperative that every teacher be an excellent teacher. No other part of the child's school experience so vitally affects him as the teachers with whom he works. The contribution that the teachers of this country have made and continue to make in developing the potentials of literally millions of children year after year and strengthening the whole structure of society is immeasurable. Because of their knowledge, their ability to impart this knowledge, and the examples they have set, aspirations have been kindled, broader visions have been acquired, and the unique talents of pupils have been cultivated to the end that they have become strong, effective citizens who have met and carried responsibilities and have moved democracy forward. For this reason, everything possible should be done to raise to the highest possible level the selection, training, retraining, and support of the teacher.

The necessity for sound liberal arts training for the teacher and for specialization in one or more subject fields at the undergraduate level is recognized. The standards of the teaching profession cannot be less than the standards of the other professions, which it helps to build. At the same time, it is of vital importance that in getting knowledge, the teacher at the same time acquire understanding of how to transmit that knowledge to learners and of the nature of the lives of those with whom he will work.

It is essential that there be close and mutually helpful relations between institutions of higher education and the schools, particularly in the preparation of teachers. Intern service, practice teaching, curriculum development, and inservice education are all parts of the picture. In these dynamic times, when instruction must be moved ahead, members of the teaching profession must know the latest and best in their fields. Inservice courses conducted by the school system preferably or by the colleges are a necessity. Incidentally, educational television has proved to be an excellent means for disseminating new information, new concepts, and new teaching methods.

Democracy in its truest sense should be exemplified in the organization and operation of the school, for the school is a community of people—children, youth, and adults; pupils, parents, and teachers—working together for the common purpose of education. Buildings, books, and budgets; policies, practices, and procedures; money, materials, and methods; all the mechanisms and devices of school organization and operation are but means. The realities of the school are the intricate webs of psychological relationships between people. On these invisible lines of mutual confidence, understanding, and respect, or in unfortunate situations, lines of suspicion, doubts, and frustrations, learning is transmitted, visions are kindled, and attitudes are formed. The school that unnecessarily violates or disregards any of the basic tenets of democracy falls short of one of its highest purposes. The true character of the school and the manner in which it performs its functions may well leave more lasting impressions on the lives of young people than any verbalizations of concepts and ideals, no matter how frequently uttered or eloquently expressed.

That school works best where everyone can present his viewpoint, can share in the planning of programs and meetings, and can enjoy the feeling that comes from knowing that he has been a "builder."

> Gone is the builder's temple,
> Crumbled into the dust;
> Low lies each stately pillar,
> Food for consuming rust.
> But the temple the teacher builded
> Will last while the ages roll;
> For that beautiful unseen temple
> Was a child's immortal soul.[4]

It is imperative that students practice democracy. Democracy becomes reality to students when they recognize the rights of others in daily classroom work and in the school yard; work together on classroom projects; play together in games or on teams; sing or play together in orchestras, bands, or choruses; serve on student councils and safety patrols; join with others in drawing up and complying with school regulations and codes of dress and good grooming; engage in "clean-up, fix-up, paint-up campaigns"; contribute to the March of Dimes, United Fund, UNICEF, Junior Red Cross, public school health funds, and Goodwill Industries clothing collections; participate in neighborhood improvement projects or Civil Defense; and donate their services to hospitals and welfare agencies.

In both elementary and secondary grades children develop understanding of the meaning of democracy as they see, hear, and read about history in the making; debate, without rancor, controversial

---

[4] Anonymous. "The Builder." *Masterpieces of Religious Verse.* (Edited by James Dalton Morrison.) New York: Harper & Brothers, 1948. p. 504.

issues; and search for their roles in the world picture. Their studies are supplemented and enriched by visits to courts, municipal service agencies, centers of business and industry, museums, institutes, and exhibitions; by discussions and presentations of civic, governmental, professional, labor, business, and industrial leaders on classroom radio and television programs and in talks before classes and assemblies; by the study of election procedures and the experimental use of voting machines; and by attendance at forums and lectures.

Those who speak disparagingly of American youth do wrong. If today's world seems to be in a confused and unfortunate state, it is certain that youth did not make it so. What critics of youth too often fail to recognize is the good wrought by youth in times of crisis and in times of peace. All too frequently the headlines highlight the shortcomings of the few and disregard the notable achievements and the sterling qualities of the many.

The primary purpose of the public schools is development of effective citizens—citizens who uphold American ideals and who act in accordance with the social and moral standards that characterize democracy. It is important that students become engineers, artists, lawyers, craftsmen, teachers, and distinguished members of other professional and highly skilled groups; it is even more important that they become effective citizens who will perpetuate democracy.

In building democratic citizens students, teachers, and principals must work together. Each student should be led, with firmness and fairness, to understand that—

> Every member of the staff is genuinely interested in and concerned about his welfare.
>
> He has direct responsibility for helping to set standards of acceptable conduct.
>
> He must respect different points of view and work with different groups for a common purpose.
>
> He is responsible for knowing what is considered desirable conduct in and about the school.
>
> Democracy demands that there be recognized leaders who represent and act for the community.
>
> He must respect and obey regulations made by democratically constituted groups, even though he may not agree with the majority.

It is imperative that the board of education be the direct representative of the people. Probably no other body carries greater responsibility for the schools than the board of education, which is the direct representative of the people. The board of education makes the policies that determine the program through which information is acquired and through which in great measure the character and attitude of the individual are built. The ultimate security of the nation is based upon the beliefs, commitments, and competencies of its people.

Through their leadership, boards of education must maintain the schools' commitment to democracy. They must use the full strength of their localities, but in using this strength, they must not be unduly swayed by pressure groups. If local control of public education is to continue, the will of the people in the community as a whole must be translated by the school board into policies and implemented by the professional staff in operational programs. While education is recognized as a state responsibility and federal aid to education is essential, these governmental authorities must not take over the functions of local school boards.

Too frequently the service and sacrifice of school board members are overlooked or treated lightly. Their rewards are seldom in the form of public acclaim. Rather, school board members are rewarded by knowing that they have played a part in strengthening the public schools and in building national wisdom, morality, and achievement. The policies formulated and adopted by school boards are implemented by their executive officer or officers and staff members. In essence school board responsibilities are related to such basic problems and issues as—

Providing the best possible education for every child, youth, or adult who attends the public school.

Providing the best teachers and other staff members who can be secured.

Planning school organization, instructional programs, and personnel policies with and through the professional and nonprofessional staff.

Providing the best possible school plant facilities, supplies, equipment, and other aids to education.

Keeping informed of educational needs and abreast of educational developments.

Keeping parents and other citizens informed of the school program and giving careful consideration to public opinion expressed at appropriate meetings or through other proper channels.

Serving as the final authority in dealing with issues which cannot be resolved through administrative channels.

Securing adequate financial support for the schools.

Providing leadership that will give dignity to the teaching profession and to the educational process and that will engender trust and confidence in public education.

It is imperative that the community and its schools work together. The schools are dependent upon the community for financial support, moral support, technical advice, educational aids, supplies, equipment, and services of many types. The community, including its businesses and industries, is dependent upon the schools for workers, purchasers of goods, taxpayers, church members, voters, makers of better communities, builders of better homes, and those who make life for others and for themselves richer and fuller—in short, the citizens.

The relationship between the school and the community is like a two-way street with signposts marked "understanding," "appreciation," and "cooperation." All who move along this street express a considerable measure of democracy in action. When a need is recognized, action necessary to meet this need is taken. To illustrate:

An advisory council made up of representatives of industry and labor works with the school in planning vocational, technical, and occupational courses for youth and adults.

Representatives of instrument and electronics industries assist the schools in setting up programs in instrumentation and automation, in securing equipment, and in placing graduates in jobs.

A municipal department of recreation provides teachers and the school board makes 30 junior high school buildings available for extended evening recreation for teenagers.

A great city orchestra permits students to attend rehearsals and provides student concerts at reduced prices.

An art museum, a science institute, a commercial museum, and an academy of natural science make facilities available for instructional purposes.

Radio-television stations make time available to acquaint the community with pressing educational issues and for instructional purposes. In one large city, a great station has provided time and services for one radio and one television instructional program a day for more than twenty years.

The Committee for Economic Development and Americans for the Competitive Enterprise System assist the schools with programs in economics.

Art museums and settlement music schools provide tuition for talented students.

The United Fund and Junior Red Cross arrange for student volunteer services in hospitals and other welfare institutions.

The merchants association of a great city cooperates in planning and implementing school-work programs in distributive education. Banks, business houses, and industries do the same in the field of cooperative office education. In one great city, student earnings in such programs are far in excess of $1 million.

The Municipal Youth Conservation Commission in a large city hires students recommended by the schools to work in the city parks after school.

The boys in a city high school located in a slum area contribute a few pennies each to help defray the hospital expenses of a woman injured in a street accident.

Local foundations help support programs of the high horizons type.

A civic committee comes to a high school to teach students about problems and issues pertaining to a general election.

Municipal health clinics cooperate with school personnel in providing dental and medical services for children who need remedial services.

The Heart Association provides instructors for students in advanced science classes held after school hours.

A great automobile company provides engines for use in automotive shops.

The Federal Bar Association arranges for student visits to courts.

A great city newspaper has for 20 years been paying half the cost of an annual music, art, and physical education extravaganza in which 3,000 to 5,000 students participate as performers.

Churches in many communities where rapidly growing enrollments have exceeded the capacities of school plants make their facilities available, at nominal cost, for use as temporary classrooms.

Businessmen, believing that education is a sound investment, actively support legislation that leads to school tax increases.

City planning commissions cooperate in securing school sites and in planning of school buildings.

Civic agencies assist with school surveys.

The parent-teacher association has as its primary purposes the interpretation of the instructional program and the development of understanding and cooperation between home and school. In most large school systems all parent-teacher associations are joined together in a central council. The board of education frequently provides office space and secretarial help for the council.

Community councils invariably place school improvement at the top of their lists of goals.

Although headlines too often feature scare stories, newspapers on the whole are friends of education and are giving the school invaluable aid.

These many illustrations no more than suggest how school work and community life are interdependent. The structure of the school, its support, its program, and its operation are deeply rooted in community life. Elementary traits of democracy—goodwill, neighborliness, fair play, courage, tolerance, patience, and open-minded inquiry make lasting imprints on the characters of young people as they gain understanding of problems and issues in community life and identify themselves with things that really count. If the schools have failed, they have failed only in reaching ideals. It is imperative that their achievements be recognized and that their efforts be given full support. The schools have stood and continue to stand as great wellsprings of freedom, equality, and self-government.

IMPERATIVE

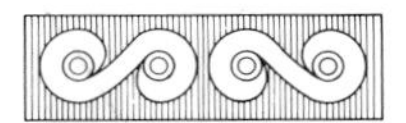

8 · TO MAKE INTELLIGENT USE OF NATURAL RESOURCES

The need for better use of natural resources and better conservation measures is imperative. This need is dramatically expressed by—

Pollution of streams with refuse from great cities and industrial plants

Wanton destruction of wild game and bird life

Raw, ugly scars on the landscape left by the strip miner

Deep, yellow gullies that stand out like bare, open wounds in badly cultivated and poorly managed fields

City streets and fertile farmlands submerged in muddy flood waters

Thousands of children playing in the back alleys and on the city streets for lack of playgrounds and open parks

Clouds of smoke and smog hanging over great centers of population and polluting the air people breathe

Particles of soil blown from parched fields that cloud the sky during the dry summer months

Lowering water tables

Severe restrictions on the use of water throughout the summer months in the country's largest city

Acres of abandoned automobiles blighting the landscape on the perimeter of nearly every town and city

Long lines of heavily-laden grocery carts emerging from chain stores in huge shopping centers

Tremendous increases in the use of physical energy by a dynamic culture

Seemingly endless construction of houses, offices, and schools that call for an ever-growing amount of materials.

ALL THE PEOPLE

The challenge set out in bold relief by these and other equally dramatic illustrations of man's dependence on natural resources is extended to all people—to the city dweller as well as the farmer, the lumberman, and the miner; to the office worker as well as to the industrialist and the manufacturer; to the legislator as well as to the teacher, the conservationist, and the land manager; and to the mature adult citizen as well as to the child in the classroom, the scout at camp, and the teenager with a fishing pole beside a mountain stream.

The natural resources of this country are entrusted to all the people. All are dependent upon them, and all share responsibility for their development and use. Decisions made and actions taken by each individual in some measure affect all others. Whether resources are used now and in the future with clear understanding and considered judgment or with ignorance and indifference depends upon the wisdom, the commitment to broad common purposes, and the feeling of responsibility for individual and group action of all people. The basic question that confronts people everywhere—and educators in particular—is whether or not in this crucial period of history the management and control of this nation's natural resources can continue to be entrusted to all the people in keeping with the essence and spirit of democracy or whether continued abuses and sheer needs will demand that regulatory measures be imposed by a central authority to safeguard an uninformed, selfish, and disinterested generation against its own careless, thoughtless, and wanton acts.

THE SCHOOL'S RESPONSIBILITY

In the use of natural resources, as in all other aspects of democratic life, the tenets of democracy demand that all people be responsible for decision and action and that they be fully informed and know what they are about. Without such knowledge and understanding and without acceptance of individual responsibility, the processes of free self-government in any and all dimensions of society cannot survive. The schools cannot and should not be burdened with the responsibility of resolving all problems of society and correcting all its ills. But in keeping with the fundamental purpose of public education, *it is imperative that the schools accept a large measure of responsibility for transmitting and inculcating into the minds and spirits of the young people they serve an understanding of the natural resources upon which the very life of this nation depends, an understanding of the growing demands made upon these resources by a dynamic culture, and an understanding of the policies and procedures essential for careful and considerate use.*

Everywhere one looks there is evidence of an abundance of natural resources, and everywhere—in homes, neighborhoods, and communities—there are illustrations of thoughtless and careless use of resources. Opportunities for objective lessons in the nature and use of natural resources lie everywhere. And yet in great measure they are overlooked, while a generation of children go through school, reach adulthood, and take their places in community life with but little sense of responsibility for the care and use of natural resources and but limited understanding of their importance to their own existence and to the well-being of their country.

PERSONAL IDENTITY

Perhaps the greatest obstacle to making more intelligent use of natural resources lies in the lack of personal identity with resources —with land, with water, with timber, with wildlife, and with the natural beauty of the landscape. Conservation is regarded by most people, even by many teachers, as an abstraction—as something that should be left to the government, to well intentioned people with missionary spirits, or to some mystical power that will ensure that each succeeding year will be better than the one before without any effort or concern on their part. Natural resources are taken for granted; they are usually available as far as the individual is concerned at the time and place he needs them. He feels an unmistakably clear personal identity with a natural resource only when some unusual circumstance occurs—when the muddy waters from a flooded valley inundate his farmlands and encroach upon his home, when a drought suddenly limits his presumedly inexhaustible supply of water, or when a smog-laden atmosphere burns his eyes and blurs his vision or aggravates a lung infection and sends him to the hospital.

The indifferent attitude of American people toward natural resources can be attributed in part to historical circumstances. As the early settler in his westward march from the Atlantic seaboard reached the crest of the Alleghenies and from this vantage point viewed the wide expanse of virgin forest, observed an abundance of bird life and wildlife, and saw clear streams of water flowing down hundreds of ravines and valleys to form great rivers, it seemed inconceivable that they could ever be exhausted or contaminated. In fact, the forests and wildlife were obstacles to be overcome by the early settler as he approached the all-important task of building a home and raising a food supply for his family. Trees were cut and the logs burned to clear open fields, and vigilance and persistent effort were required to keep wild game and birds from devouring the scanty crops growing amidst the stumps in the clearings. It was a struggle of man for existence against the forces and elements of nature. Rather than attaching value to these priceless resources, the settlers regarded them as threats to their very existence. And if at some point the supply seemed less than abundant, the settler had only to move over the crest of the next mountain to new, fresh, untamed territory to begin all over again. It was only in the semiarid regions and the deserts that men felt a concern for water supplies; and fresh air, in abundance everywhere, was taken for granted. Only a dreamer or one with unusual prophetic vision even a half century ago could have envisioned a time when the atmosphere would become so laden with impurities that health and life itself would be threatened.

Growing demands on natural resources fed by the forces of population growth, cultural change, and rising levels of living have silently but persistently crept forward like a great glacial movement while the individual's focus of attention has been on his own survival and well-being. It is only as individual interests are seen in a broader perspective and penetrate the stream of social consciousness that serious thought has been given to the manner in which resources are used and to ways of conserving them so that American life in the future will not be impaired.

GROWING DEMANDS

American life grows and becomes fuller and richer in almost every dimension with each passing decade. A century ago there were about 31 million people in the United States; now there are more than 191 million; and experts predict that the population in this country may increase to more than 360 million by the end of the next four decades. Thus, measured by present standards of quantity and quality of goods and services needed, demands made on the productive capacities of the soil, on water resources, on metallic and mineral resources, on forest and fuel supplies, and on space for living will increase by more than 70 percent by the year 2000. The magnitude of these demands of a growing population on the natural resources of the country, however, cannot be projected on the basis of an increasing population alone. Levels of living can reasonably be expected to rise, and the nature and quality of goods and services can be expected to change.

Goods and services known only to the rich in one generation become necessities in the next. Economists predict that the per capita consumer expenditure will increase by almost 50 percent during the next 20 years and by more than 100 percent by the end of the century. Expenditures are likely to increase for recreation, education, travel, personal and medical care, automobiles, household appliances, and housing. Between 1960 and the year 2000, 50 million housing units will be needed. Present trends indicate that these units will be equipped in a manner that will increase the demands on many types of natural resources. To illustrate these increasing requirements:

> [Many families] now owning refrigerators with an 11 cubic-foot capacity, shelving in the door, a large freezing compartment and automatic defrosting were satisfied, not so long ago, with a model with only 7 cubic-foot capacity, no freezer and no defroster.
>
> . . . . Only 7 percent of all households own dishwashers, only 10 percent have food waste disposers, and only 20 percent clothes dryers. A widely acceptable automatic ironer is still to reach the market. Other appliances may not even be on the drawing board.[1]

It is difficult to visualize the demands on natural resources created by cultural change. To illustrate:

> An urban family uses about six times as much water as a farm family that draws its water from a well. About 3 gallons of water are used to flush a toilet; about 30 gallons to fill a typical sunken bathtub 6 inches in depth; an even larger quantity to clean a load of clothing in an automatic washing machine. A typical 1,000-ton air conditioning unit, of the kind that is favored in cafeterias, uses up enough water to meet the daily needs of more than 30,000 people.
>
> In round figures it requires about 50,000 gallons of water to produce a ton of paper, 100,000 gallons to produce a ton of copper,

[1] Landsberg, Hans H. *Natural Resources for U.S. Growth.* Washington, D.C.: Resources for the Future, 1964. p. 64.

> 200,000 to produce a ton of rayon, 320,000 to produce a ton of aluminum, 600,000 to produce a ton of synthetic rubber.[2]

In 1960 there were about 59 million automobiles operated by their owners. If present trends continue, the number of automobiles owned and operated by individuals will increase to 120 million by 1980 and to more than 240 million by the year 2000. In other words, by the end of this century there will be four times as many automobiles on the streets and highways of this country as there are at the present time.[3]

The tremendous demands made on natural resources by just this one segment of the economic enterprise can be visualized by looking at the materials required for construction and the fuel needed for operation. "The average automobile produced in 1960 weighed something like 3,500 pounds, of which 2,400 pounds was steel, 600 cast iron, 60 aluminum, and the remainder other materials." [4] Automobiles in 1960 consumed about 40 billion gallons of fuel, buses 1 billion gallons, the railroads about 4 billion gallons, and airplanes about 2 billion gallons.[5]

Wherever one looks in the total industrial enterprise and in the total culture of this country, prospects for increasing demands on natural resources are of gigantic proportions—whether it be for water, fiber, wood products, minerals, electrical energy, or space for living. Some of this demand will be eased by scientific discoveries, new methods of production, and the development of new materials. For instance, it has been estimated that had corn yields remained at the level common in the decade of the forties, it would have taken 100 million acres to produce the crop grown on 57 million acres in 1962. But despite the application of man's creative and inventive genius to the use of natural resources and to the production and distribution of goods, the growing demands on natural resources by a rapidly increasing population and a rising level of living make it imperative that all the people be made fully aware of the necessity for making the best possible use of resources.

VALUES AND UNDERSTANDING

As one seriously and soberly inquires what it is that the people of this country want to accomplish through education during the

---

[2] Herber, Lewis. *Crisis in Our Cities.* Englewood Cliffs, N.J.: Prentice-Hall, 1965. p. 92.

[3] Landsberg, Hans H., *op. cit.,* p. 53.

[4] *Ibid.,* p. 59.

[5] *Ibid.,* p. 54.

years immediately ahead, he finds that sane and sensible development and use of the natural resources of the country holds a position of high priority in the cluster of purposes people want to achieve. Natural resources—in particular, soil, water, and air—are vital to the sustenance of life itself; if they are abused, misused, or in short supply in any country, levels of living drop and want and poverty haunt the people. Waste of natural resources, whether through neglect, wanton destruction, or ignorance, robs people of potential for good living.

The problems and issues that constitute the substance of an instructional program on the use of natural resources are broader and go far deeper than the isolated actions of individuals. Like most other educational problems, they represent complex forces deeply rooted in the culture of the times and are part and parcel of it. Consequently, it becomes highly important that the people of each age, each generation, each decade, and, in particular, each period of rapid cultural change thoroughly understand existing conditions, identify persistent problems, and make intelligent approaches to resolving them.

The schools are challenged as never before to acquaint a growing pupil population with a background of essential information pertaining to the conservation of natural resources and their relationship to the total culture of the country and of the world. But more than the acquisition of factual information is needed if this teaching is to be effective in adult life where conservation problems are met at policy-forming, decision-making, and operational levels. Attitudes must be developed, values must be cultivated, and personal commitments must be made that will stand up well in the stress and strain of the social, economic, and political life of the adult world.

Martin's vivid description of the controversy that raged and the difficulties encountered as attempts were made to construct a water storage reservoir in the Adirondacks just outside New York City illustrates the problems and processes of community action in making use of natural resources. As these common efforts were made to improve and to increase the water supply for a great center of population, private and selfish interests were pitted against the common good. In the hearings on the proposed reservoir, representatives from 36 civic and special interest groups appeared in opposition to the plan. Only 8 such groups supported it.[6] The leadership task in such an undertaking is tremendously difficult and frustrating. Yet

---

[6] Martin, Roscoe C. *Water for New York; A Study in State Administration of Water Resources.* Syracuse, N.Y.: Syracuse University Press, 1960.

despite the difficulties that were encountered in this particular instance and that will undoubtedly be encountered in other instances, a way must be found to resolve such problems. This way will be through understanding.

Issues pertaining to the use of natural resources are primarily political. The problems of engineering in the development of a water supply for a city, elimination of river pollution, or prevention of air pollution or soil erosion are less difficult than securing the commitment and support of the people in the regions affected by these measures. The crux of the resource problem to an increasing degree lies in the social order, in the values to which people adhere, and in the patterns of social interaction which govern the use of resources.

If a generation of children are to understand how to use the natural resources of this country more intelligently, they must be taught to look beyond the work of the conservation technician to the legal institutions of land ownership; to the values of society; to the hard, cold facts of economics; and to the basic needs of the people.

> The challenge that confronts the schools in conservation education is accentuated by a time factor. It is not children who destroy the forests, waste the fertility of the soil, despoil streams, and mar the landscape with unnecessary blemishes. This is the work of adults—the marginal farmer who, from lack of understanding or because of economic pressures, handles his land badly and sees its fertility slipping away from him year after year; the strip miner who is so hard pressed in making ends meet that he moves on to another operation without going to the trouble or expense of repairing the injury he has done to the land; the careless hunter or camper who drops a match or a burning cigarette that starts a forest fire on an important watershed; the politician who, because of special interests, resists building a necessary flood control dam or sewage disposal plant; and the average citizen who, because of indifference, lethargy, or sheer laziness, does not concern himself with the problems of conservation and fails to carry his full share of responsibility for shaping the policy that governs the care and use of resources.[7]

Each year, increasing urbanization removes more and more people from direct contact and experiences with nature—with water, wild life, soil, forests, birds, and the beauty of an unblemished countryside. As the distance between the original source of a natural resource and the lives of the people who so fully depend on it increases through urbanization and industrialization, it becomes more and more important that the schools bridge this void in understand-

[7] American Association of School Administrators. *Conservation—In the People's Hands.* Washington, D.C.: the Association, 1964. p. 10.

ing and information through an appropriate and effective educational program. With three-quarters or more of the total population living in urban communities, the citizen of the city—rather than the farmer, the lumberman, or the miner—will largely determine whether natural resources are wisely or unwisely used.

It is imperative that children be led to fully understand that—

Conservation is not a sentimental hobby but a serious concern vitally related to their own households and ways of living and firmly established in the laws of nature.

The natural resources of the country—particularly soil, water, air, oil, gas, and minerals—are not inexhaustible, and the demands being placed upon them may become so great in a relatively short period of time that the use of some resources will be limited.

Conservation is not merely saving, but planning for intelligent and efficient use.

Much of the depletion of the natural resources of this country has been unnecessary; it has come from ignorance, shortsightedness, greediness, selfishness, and the lack of full comprehension of the importance of this natural heritage to the well-being of all people.

Those who are privileged to be in control of natural resources—whether on a large scale or a limited basis—have responsibility in a form not unlike a stewardship for passing this natural heritage along to those who will follow in as good or better condition than they received it.

Extravagant use or waste leading to the depletion of a natural resource is a grave disservice to the country as a whole, to the community in which one lives, and to the individual himself.

Actions that lead to unnecessary depletion of resources, or unwise use of them, are often the result of attitudes toward and conflicts in cultural values. It is clear that water is unnecessarily wasted, that topsoil blows away during dry summer months, that gullies emerge on hillsides, that floods inundate river valley farms and destroy communities, and that wastes from cities and industrial plants pollute streams. But when these facts are checked against underlying cultural values, it is also clear that many decisions have been made without due regard to the facts.

Conservation problems and issues often emerge with political and economic overtones. Action calling for their solution involves people on a community, county, state, or regional basis. Consideration of these problems must be broad and comprehensive. Each child has an individual responsibility for the use of natural resources at the present time, and this responsibility will continue to grow in importance as he becomes older and takes a more active part in community life as the head of a family or as a leader in some phase of social, economic, or governmental life in his community.

TEACHING RESOURCES

The contributions that the schools can make to the solution of conservation problems will not be in the nature of great undertakings. They must be simple, direct, and immediate. Pupils must be involved in activities that convey meanings and give satisfactions. Time must be allowed for growth and maturation in the organization of factual information, the weighing of alternatives, and the forming of judgments. The concepts, beliefs, and convictions formed in youthful minds must be clear enough, firm enough, and tough enough to stand up under the strenuous pressures of adult life.

The imaginative and well-informed teacher will find a thousand ways to teach conservation. For example, in the study of a mineral he may help children learn its value, its use, its chemical properties, how it is mined, what substitutes can be used for it, how it was formed, how much exists, how the land is affected through the mining process, and ways to eliminate unnecessary waste. A teacher and pupils in an elementary classroom may make a weather chart, build a birdhouse, sprout seeds in a bottle of water, keep and feed a hamster or a rabbit, measure the waste of water from a leaking faucet, plant a tree, grow a garden, or—if circumstances permit—follow a nature trail through the woods. The important point in any instruction in conservation is that children learn how to observe, how to collect facts, and how to interpret facts and learn to sense a close affinity between natural resources, human life, and the totality of all nature.

Teachers and pupils in a rural school in the open country or in a school located in a sprawling suburb have a decided advantage. Many of the factors and forces directly and positively related to the use and conservation of natural resources lie all about the school as an open book. Every growing plant, every plot of grass, every level plain and sloping hillside, every stream and pond, and every change in the weather—the stones, the soil, the color and structure of leaves, the sun and the clouds, the wind and the storms, the birds and the insects, the water supply and the sewage disposal system, the domesticated animals on the farms and the small wild creatures in the woods, the patch of violets in a shady nook and the row of hollyhocks along the driveway—all are readily available to be studied, to be seen in relationship to each other, to be enjoyed, and to be understood and accepted as a part of all life and of man's very existence.

But in great measure this tremendous laboratory for research, for study, for enjoyment, for stimulating the imaginations and creative energies of children, and for shaping their attitudes and values is taken for granted and overlooked; its potential is ignored, disregarded, or treated lightly. Live, rich, and vital teaching and learning experiences are left by the wayside while children are pushed through vicarious experiences inside the classroom that many times have little or no relevance to the realities of life which the instructional program should help them understand.

One could well ask why this great teaching and learning laboratory is not used. The answer perhaps lies in the established purposes of the instructional program, in the preparation of teachers, and in the expectancies of the citizens of the community. Historical circumstances have led people to believe that children will pick up and learn incidentally all they need to know about the natural life of their neighborhoods and communities, that this need not be a part of the regular school program, that the use of natural resources is something that will be taken care of in an appropriate manner through economic enterprise, and that information gleaned from printed pages is more respectable and has greater worth than information acquired from the natural life about the school.

When the people in a community seriously address themselves to shaping and giving substance to an instructional program that will help the children in school comprehend the basic principles of the use and conservation of natural resources, this purpose will be clearly reflected in the objectives of the educational program, in the preparation of teachers, in the location and development of the school site, in the design of the school plant, in the character of instructional methods, and in the appraisal of pupil progress toward the ends the school is expected to reach. Where such policy exists, it will be as commonplace to see teachers and pupils working together around a pond on the school site, along a little rivulet, or in a school garden or community park as to see them working in the science laboratory, in the library, or in the classroom. One will not replace the other; neither will a higher priority be given to learning that takes place in one situation as compared to another. Rather, the emphasis will be on using the best possible resources and the best possible circumstances to accomplish the end in view. It is in this manner that the educational program will be strengthened, that a new dimension will be added to it, and that children's understanding of the nature and use of natural resources will be cultivated and brought to a higher level of maturity.

IN CITY CLASSROOMS

But the circumstances confronting the pupils and teachers in the classrooms of the school building in the heart of a great city are different. Here, more often than not, the school building is surrounded by streets laden with moving vehicles, with ugly patches of blacktop, and with noise and congestion. Grassy plots, flowering gardens, majestic trees, attractive shrubs, ponds and pools, birds and wildlife, and broad acres of growing green plants and grassland are not parts of the school environment. To visualize or suggest the possibility of substantial numbers of school children in such circumstances being given firsthand acquaintance and experience with such outdoor teaching and learning laboratories is but idle daydreaming.

Yet it is in just such situations that the necessity for teaching young people the principles, processes, and relationships essential to intelligent use and conservation of natural resources is greatest. It is in these circumstances that the greatest skill in instruction, the fullest commitment of the teaching staff, and the most discerning insight into school policy and purposes are required and must be provided. While the challenge is formidable, it is by no means insurmountable. As the prince in the ancient legend took the broken sword that the cringing knight had jealously broken in two and discarded and turned the tide of the battle, so must administrators and teachers—even when the circumstances are difficult—meet the challenge of instilling in the minds and hearts of a generation of young people the understanding and commitment necessary to use the natural resources of this country intelligently.

As is true in all other facets of the instructional program, individual initiative, imagination, and creative thought will find the way best suited to the circumstances in developing a vital program in conservation use. Like the prince in the legend, administrators and teachers will use whatever resources exist to the best possible advantage. They, too, may find opportunities for stimulating experiences outside as well as inside the classroom; for example, the movement of cargoes of metals, food, fuel, fibers, and lumber along the wharves and docks at the waterfront as they are loaded and unloaded from trains and ships that serve as lifelines between the consuming cities and the productive hinterland.

Comprehension of the nature and amounts of commodities used by a great city may be developed by observing the flow of materials into and out of industrial plants, department stores, food stores, and fueling stations. The pupils in the large city school are in closer proximity to the causes for pollution of rivers and the atmosphere than their country cousins. With powers for observation sharpened, they can easily observe the pressures for living space; the causes for congestion; the sources of noise, dust, and smoke; and at the same time, properly guided, they can become sensitive to the measures gradually being instituted to meet and deal with these common problems of urbanization. They can become familiar with charges against the family budget for their water supply, for sewage disposal, for collection and removal of garbage, for control of smoke, and for the creation and maintenance of parks and playgrounds.

Children in the urban schools can be led to see how the supply and use of natural resources directly affects them. The harmony, the beauty, and the all-encompassing relationships in the balance of nature can be portrayed in the biological laboratory in the city school with as much clarity as the properties and relationships of the inanimate elements handled with great success in the chemistry laboratories. But to accomplish this end it undoubtedly will be necessary to give greater thought to and perhaps make larger expenditures in developing biology laboratories. Furthermore, substantial improvements may be made in the design and location of the school plant.

School administrators who feel a deep commitment to transmit to a generation of children a sense of the beauty, the harmony, and the wonder of life—whether in a growing plant, a small animal, or the complex relationship between the inhabitants of a great city and the natural resources of a nation—may provide a flowering garden filled with beauty in place of the small plot of blacktop that inadequately serves as outdoor play space for the children attending the city school. Through planning and design, the needs for play space might be more adequately met on the roof of the building or in an appropriately designed space in the interior, freeing the limited outdoor space that is available for this added instructional facility. It may be that laboratories will be designed where elementary children can gain rich and vital experiences through keeping and caring for small animals and fowls or that classrooms will be designed where growing plants in unobtrusive window boxes become a functional part of the interior classroom environment. And undoubtedly tremendous progress can be made in acquainting young people with the wonders, relationships, and properties of natural resources through slides, films, tapes, and various types of recordings.

In developing an effective program for teaching children how to know, how to appreciate, and how to use natural resources with more intelligence, it is imperative that administrators and teachers commit themselves to this purpose, believe that it is possible, give this instruction appropriate priority, assign someone responsibility for seeing that it is done, and give the work in this area of the instructional program appropriate recognition in the evaluation of pupil achievement and the quality of the educational program.

IMPERATIVE

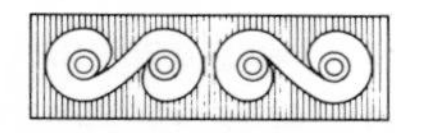

9 · TO MAKE THE BEST USE OF LEISURE TIME

The United States has led in the development of an industrial and scientific society, with its advantages and compensations broadly distributed and with rising levels of living for most people. No small part of the gain has been and will be increased leisure time. Working hours are shorter; the span of life is longer; and custom and legislative action cause many people to retire while their minds are still active and their bodies still vigorous. Furthermore, with the increased use of machines, automation, and new sources of energy, leisure time will continue to increase. It has been estimated that about 25 percent of the total national time was devoted to leisure in 1900 and about 34 percent in 1950. Projected estimates indicate that by the year 2000 about 38 percent of the total national time will be leisure time.[1]

There is perhaps no greater educational need in this country now than to learn to make the best possible use of human resources.

> Clearly this throws us back on education in the broadest sense. Maybe, in the phrase of Professor MacLuhan of Toronto, we must

[1] American Academy of Political and Social Science. *Leisure in America: Blessing or Curse?* (Edited by James C. Charlesworth.) Philadelphia: the Academy, 1964. p. 10.

Explanatory note: In computing these data, a national time budget estimate was made by multiplying the total number of inhabitants in the country by 24 hours for each day and again by 365 days of the year. This total number of hours for all people in the nation was broken down into the following general categories: sleep, work, school, housekeeping, nonsleeping hours of preschool population, and personal care. The remainder is assumed to be largely leisure time.

> no longer think of "earning a living" so much as "learning a living," seeing our lives as chances not only to gain our daily bread and secure our physical survival, but as "values of soul making," in Keats' splendid phrase.
>
> In the more leisured society we are about to face, training in all forms of excellence—in the arts, in literature, in history, in physical culture—could be the balance to any over-specialization on the technical or scientific side. Once again, we have to see this as a process in which men and women throughout their lives can use their new leisure for deepening knowledge and insight, and hence enjoyment.
>
> We already see small blossomings of this new spring—in the fabulous proliferation of serious paperback books, in art centers, theaters, museums, orchestras growing up all over our country—each capable of becoming the focus of a new and lively kind of civic education.[2]

This is not to imply that there is any central authority in a community, a state, or the nation that should attempt to control how people use their time and energies. At the groundbreaking ceremony for the John F. Kennedy Center for the Performing Arts on the banks of the Potomac, President Johnson said:

> The role of government must be a small one. No Act of Congress or Executive Order can call a great musician or poet into existence. But we can stand on the sidelines and cheer. We can maintain and strengthen an atmosphere to permit the arts to flourish, and those who have talent to use it. And we can seek to enlarge the access of all of our people to artistic creation.[3]

The use of human resources and talent is an individual matter. But if an individual chooses to waste away his time, it is a loss not only to himself but to his community and to the nation as a whole. One needs only to look about any neighborhood or community to see that a great amount of leisure time is being wasted—the lonely teen-age boy standing on a street corner; workmen at the end of the day leaning against the bar in a tavern; suburban housewives playing bridge on Wednesday afternoon; young business executives watching the tawdry, boisterous entertainment in a plush night club; a thousand cars parked around the arena on bingo night; and a displaced miner sitting idly by the window in his cottage, waiting for something to come his way. When in ignorance leisure time is wasted, the lives of individuals may become shallow and pointless, and community life blighted.

On the other hand, if an individual's sense of values and patterns of behavior are such that he uses his full time and energy to good

---

[2] Stevenson, Adlai E. "The Centrality of Education." Address given at the Honors Day Convocation, University of Illinois, Urbana-Champaign, May 1, 1964.

[3] Office of the White House Press Secretary. News release, December 2, 1964. Washington, D.C.: the White House, 1964. p. 2.

advantage, his life is likely to be richer and fuller and the community in which he lives better than it otherwise would be. This is true for child, youth, and adult. It was the people with leisure time in the cultures from which Western civilization draws many of its values, ideals, and concepts, much of its philosophy, and much of its literature who thought, wrote, debated, taught, painted, created, and invented.

Leisure time in these earlier civilizations—available to the leaders and creators of cultural foundations, Archimedes, Aristotle, Euripides, Plato, Ptolemy, and Solon—usually was supported by enslaved populations. Leisure time was a luxury for the few. Now, in this country, leisure time is available to people in all walks of life—the day laborer as well as the landowner, the small business man as well as the leader of a great industrial enterprise, and the housewife living in a modest bungalow as well as the wealthy socialite in a luxurious penthouse. It is in this margin of time and energy beyond what is required for the necessities of living that the potential lies for creating clearer insights into human behavior; firmer concepts of the meaning of freedom; more just methods of government; nobler concepts of architecture; and great literature, great art, great music, great sculpture, and great humanitarian ideals.

Perplexing problems of this age that call loudly for solution sorely need the human energy that has been released in the form of leisure time. The threats of war, racial strife, social tensions, crime, air pollution, unemployment, poverty, disease, and famine are but a few of the great problems which confront the people of this country and peoples all over the world. There are perhaps no easy solutions to these difficult problems, but as the minds of men are directed toward developing better understanding of their causes and effects and devising better means of dealing with them, their ill effects will be diminished in some degree, civilization will have advanced to a little higher level, and the lives of people will be better.

The Peace Corps, the Neighborhood Youth Corps, and the National Teachers Corps are illustrations of steps that have recently been taken at the national level to divert leisure time of individuals to useful purposes. When in a comparable manner leisure time of people in thousands of local communities is directed away from aimless drift and toward important purposes, there is good reason for believing that tensions will be lessened, tenement districts in large cities less common, and the ills that beset people of all ages and in all walks of life less intense. Such is the hope and commitment of education.

It is not the intent here to suggest regimentation of leisure time activities; such a purpose, if achieved, would destroy the essence of leisure time; neither is it the intent to suggest specific ways of harnessing this new social potential and directing it to particular ends. Rather, the intent is to suggest a wider range of choices in the use of leisure time. Leisure time should mean time used in a manner of one's own choosing. But if the range of opportunities is limited, cast at a low level, or tuned to cheap and tawdry concepts and ideas, leisure time can become frightening, boring, and restraining and may deteriorate into idleness, discontent, and at times even delinquency.

Can the schools accept the challenge to train people to use leisure time intelligently? They have done so. Worthy use of leisure time was identified as one of the Seven Cardinal Principles more than forty years ago. Modest efforts initiated and sustained in the schools have been carried over into the adult life of the community. André Maurois, distinguished French author, was recently quoted in *U.S. News and World Report* as follows:

> I was struck, the first time I went to the U. S., by the number of museums, the large number of people who visited them, by the fact that there was a symphony orchestra in practically every city.
>
> People not only knew good music, but very good music. And this comes from the fact that music is taught in American schools. There are records, and the radio stations broadcast plenty of good music. So the musical education of the nation was rather better than in Europe.[4]

But now leisure time is appearing in a new and different setting and in greater proportions. With the help that local government and other agencies may provide, the efforts of the schools to teach people how to use leisure time to better advantage can be accentuated and become far-reaching through classroom instruction for children and youth and a continuing education program for adults.

The schools might make many approaches to the solution of this broad problem, but their efforts will perhaps be more rewarding if they are fitted into existing patterns of organization and the well established framework of the instructional program. Through such an approach, the schools do have opportunities for awakening in the minds of a generation of young people an awareness of the importance of leisure time to each and every individual and to society as a whole and, at the same time, cultivating values, habits, and practices that will lead them individually and collectively to better use of leisure time. This can be done through—

Reading
English
Science

---

[4] Maurois, André. Quoted in "What's Right in America: As Observers Abroad See It." *U.S. News and World Report* 57:45; September 14, 1964.

Music

Graphic arts

Vocational education

Physical education

Home economics

Student government and other activities.

READING

Never before has so much effort been given to teaching reading, the foundation of learning. There is continuing effort to provide the best methods in basic reading, developmental reading, remedial reading, and speed reading. Teaching reading is not the responsibility of the elementary teacher alone. Teachers of every subject at every educational level through precept and example should emphasize the values and joys to be gleaned from the printed page. Thereupon lie essential knowledge, entertainment, inspiration, and spiritual direction.

The Great Books and great books are available for young and old. They come in costly bindings and paperbacks. They are available at every corner drugstore and newsstand and from the local public library and the bookmobile that moves around the city streets and up and down the country lanes. The service of the school itself is not limited to children and youth. The adult evening schools, the classes in English and citizenship, the TV "Operation Alphabet," the local book clubs, and many other services can be made available for those of mature years. The home also must do its share in encouraging reading, and the schools can most certainly stimulate this action. Alert and creative leaders will find many opportunities for getting more books and better books into the hands of people. To illustrate, in a recent annual fair of a home and school association of a city school in the slums it was decided to sell books for children instead of cakes and candies. The sales totaled more than $2,000.

The teacher who instills in a child a genuine love for reading has introduced him to the great minds of all ages. W. Somerset Maugham, in an interview on his ninetieth birthday, commented:

> In a great library, you get into society in the widest sense, with the huge advantage of needing no introductions and of not dreading repulses. From that great crowd you can choose what companions you please, for in these silent gatherings of the immortals there is no pride. The highest is at the service of the lowest, with a grand humility. You may speak freely with any, for books are perfectly well-

> bred and hurt no one's feelings by any discriminations. In a library you become a true citizen of the world.[5]

There are millions of people who, because of intimate acquaintances with great books gained in their leisure hours and in their busy ones as well, have nobler thoughts and larger visions. The vice-president of a city bank expressed this feeling in a simple and direct way at a recent social gathering, when he saw one of his former teachers in the group and commented in the warmest tones, "There is the man who taught me to love to read."

ENGLISH

There is perhaps no greater unifying force in all culture than a common language. It is the most important means of communication between and among people. For all who have skill to use it—and nearly everyone has some language skills—it is a ready means of gathering ideas, sharing feelings and opinions, and transmitting thoughts. In its various forms—writing, speaking, the printed page, the dramatic presentation, and simple informal conversation—it brings the minds of men together and gives unity to society as a whole. The possibilities in its use are almost boundless—limited only by skill to use it. Montaigne contended:

> The most fruitful and natural exercise of the mind, in my opinion, is conversation; I find the use of it more sweet than of any other action of life; and for that reason it is that, if I were now compelled to choose, I should sooner, I think, consent to lose my sight, than my hearing and speech.[6]

In all areas of the educational program there are opportunities for students to enter into discussion with others. Whether it be in the third-grade classroom, at the sophomore committee meeting, on the science club field trip, on the athletic field, at the school fair, or in conversation in corridors between classes, there will be sharing of opinions, questioning of decisions, enlisting of support, challenge through critical thinking, and the building of friendships. All of this is pertinent to present and future leisure hours. In every home, school, church, and neighborhood there are countless opportunities for carrying on that interchange of thought and spirit that helps men and nations to be re-created.

---

[5] Maugham, W. Somerset. "A Confidential Question." *NEA Journal* 54: 9; April 1965.

[6] Montaigne, Michel de. "Of the Art of Conference." *Great Books of the Western World.* Chicago: Encyclopaedia Britannica, 1952. Vol. 25, p. 446.

Words are used to state a fact, pose a problem, or communicate a wish; they can also serve a purpose closer to the heart's desire through the imagery and rhythm of poetry or the power and clarity of prose. The good teacher recognizes that the creative use of written language at all levels of a student's development needs encouragement. Opportunities are present in classroom work, in student publications, in clubs, in contributions to public news organs, and in other programs.

In secondary grades, creative writing groups—in addition to their essays, short stories, poetry, and plays—often work together with students of music and modern dance to produce songs, choreography, and dramatic productions for their own pleasure and for public demonstration. In the course of school life all children should be encouraged to find expression in dramatics and public speaking. Teachers and administrators sensitive to the importance of making English activities an enjoyable rather than a boring experience are turning to the little theater as well as to the school library. In the better school buildings recently constructed the little theater is common, and school principals point out that this facility is one of the most extensively used units in the entire school plant. These activities, extending from the schools into municipal recreation centers, civic centers, and little theaters, can provide pleasure and raise cultural sights for performers and audience.

It is all-important that language skills and patterns of use be introduced at an early age so they can mature as one grows older. Fitzgerald, in a letter to his daughter, wrote:

> Once one is caught up into the material world not one person in ten thousand finds the time to form literary taste, to examine the validity of philosophic concepts for himself, or to form what, for lack of a better phrase, I might call the wise and tragic sense of life.[7]

SCIENCE

"The curse that has been laid on humanity, in fable and in fact," Whitehead observed, "is, that by the sweat of its brow shall it live." [8] But science and invention have gone far in easing the weight of this burden. People now talk openly of fears that machines will take away their jobs, deprive them of the opportunity to work, and displace them from useful roles in community life. One of the most serious

---

[7] Fitzgerald, F. Scott. *The Letters of F. Scott Fitzgerald.* (Edited by Andrew Turnbull.) New York: Charles Scribner's Sons, 1963. p. 96.

[8] Whitehead, Alfred North. *The Aims of Education.* New York: Mentor Books, 1961. p. 52.

questions that confronts this age is what happens to people when they are no longer employed in earning a living and sustaining an economy.

At no point in the entire cultural spectrum is this question more pertinent than in the field of science, for it is through science and invention that man's work has been placed in a new setting and it is in science and related fields that great new challenges have been created. As men's labors have been lightened on the farms, in the mines, and in industrial plants, the need for distilling wisdom essential for guiding society from the mass of accumulated knowledge has become much greater. Undoubtedly the greatest possibility for meeting this need lies in more effective use of leisure time.

The field of science is a great commonwealth of information, of practices, of questions that stir the imaginations and creative capacities of people. It touches the life of each individual and it extends challenges to everyone if he but recognizes them. The fullest satisfactions of life come from knowing how to meet its challenges. The response of education to the world of science and technology up to the present time has been in conformity with five underlying principles. They are—

> (1) more education for more people, (2) educational booster shots in some form of continuing adult education, (3) increased production of scientists and engineers, (4) expanded vocational training, and (5) mid-career refresher training or retraining for a different specialty.[9]

No one can quarrel with these goals, but somehow they fall short of reaching that great group of people who have time that could be devoted to becoming more intimately acquainted with the great forces and patterns of nature, to experimenting in an intelligent manner with the physical forces about them that affect their daily lives, and to gaining the deep satisfactions that come from searching for basic relationships and discovering fundamental truths.

It is imperative that children be taught to read the book of life that always lies open before them. How many youngsters go to the beaches and fail to see the sea? How many people drive through the countryside and fail to see the fields and trees and streams? How many people race through life without really knowing the beauty of a sunset, the splendor of a mountain range viewed in perspective, and the delight in the fragrance of field lilies? Learning the basic principles and essentials of a disciplined science is only the first step in learning how to read and enjoy the great book of life. Somehow teachers must find ways to rise above associating learning exclusively with informa-

---

[9] Mesthene, Emmanual G. "Learning To Live with Science." *Saturday Review* 48: 16; July 17, 1965.

tion transmitted by a book, which of necessity is of a secondhand nature. The disciplines of science when thoroughly mastered can be applied in the world of everyone—in the logic of discovery, in weighing probabilities, in discarding trivial details, and in reaching for the harmony and truth that prevail.

Teachers in elementary schools, through methods uniquely adapted to the situations in which they work, are cultivating such desires and skills in young children through science clubs, fairs, exhibits, school gardens, school camps, and field trips and through collections and classifications of stones, minerals, and plant life. Interests stirred at the elementary level with appropriate stimulation and guidance become stronger at the secondary level. One who has observed teen-age youngsters working in modern biological laboratories caring for rabbits, reptiles, or guinea pigs; hatching and feeding baby chicks; and studying the growth patterns of plants; or working in physical science laboratories with the compounds of rare gases, photoelectric measurements, and velocities of particles moving in magnetic fields cannot but know that these experiences will make their lives richer and more rewarding than they otherwise might have been.

There are countless Americans who as a result of their school experiences in science have come to know the joy of living, working, and relaxing in the out-of-doors; to appreciate the beauty and wonders of nature; and to enjoy gardening, bird watching, fishing and hunting, and raising animals. Because of interest in science they have been able to interpret their environments with resultant enjoyment of leisure.

MUSIC

Music is an art—indeed, the art of the angels; the art of melody that touches every sensitive spot of the spirit; the art of the composer, the player, the listener.

Music instruction begins at the kindergarten level and progresses through all the grades. School is not only a place to study but a place to sing. Children love to sing—to sing alone or in selected groups, to sing in the classroom or to sing in the assembly, the family altar of the school. When one hears their voices lifted in harmony, he knows there are stars in their hearts; he comes to understand with the poet:

> We need love's tender lessons taught
> As only weakness can;
> God hath His small interpreters;
> The child must teach the man.[10]

---

[10] Whittier, John Greenleaf. "Child-Songs." *The Complete Poetical Works of John Greenleaf Whittier*. New York: Houghton Mifflin Co., 1894. p. 454.

From the classroom singing group it is but a step to the wonderful choruses and choirs of intermediate and junior and senior high school levels. It is but a step from the folk song of the little ones to the seniors' Tallis "Motet" with 40 independent voice parts and a score which includes all conceivable combinations.

Almost every child can learn to play a musical instrument. At the kindergarten level and through the elementary grades they can play upon bar bells, xylophones, melody flutes, zithers, and percussion instruments. Then there open up the opportunities in the elementary orchestras and the junior and senior high school bands and orchestras. Every school at any level should have one or more electric organs for use by pupils. Every school system should provide special instructors of instrumental and vocal music.

Children in most communities have many opportunities to perform at school and community concerts, at citywide festivals, and at conventions. Many communities have private musical organizations, great orchestras and bands, operatic societies, and other groups ready to cooperate in training young people and in affording them unique opportunities to enjoy good music. Most important, all children can be taught to appreciate good music readily available on records or on radio and television or through attendance at live performances. Many school systems use all these media.

The leisure hours of young and old alike will be richer and fuller if they have learned to appreciate and to enjoy good music. Music instruction in the school contributes to the preparation of tomorrow's artists and to the development of inspirational and spiritual values. Music is a universal language. If the participants in international conferences would stop now and then to sing together, they would more often come to successful agreements. Immediately after winning the International Tchaikovsky Competition in Moscow, Van Cliburn wrote:

> There are no political barriers to music. The same blood running through Americans also runs through the Soviet people and compels us to enjoy the same art. What thrills me so much is the spirit of musical unity achieved at the Tchaikovsky Competition by people of the world whose governments are at political loggerheads.[11]

GRAPHIC ARTS

Art is universal. It is as old as the human race and just as much a part of man as his eyes or his ears, or his hunger or his thirst. Instruc-

[11] Cliburn, Van. Quoted by Karl D. Ernst, in American Association of School Administrators. *Your AASA in 1958-59.* Washington, D.C.: the Association, 1959. pp. 224-25.

tion in the graphic arts is central and essential to the individual's happiness and the nation's well-being. Schools must and do realize that the younger generation is looking for something at once more demanding and more genuinely satisfying than what passes for happiness by current standards. Schools must and do know that—

> It is the glory and good of Art,
> That Art remains the one way possible
> Of speaking truth. . . .[12]

It is imperative that all schools have comprehensive and effective art programs. An effective program of art education is based on recognition that—

> Every individual has the need and capacity to express his reactions to the world in which he lives. Not only do needs and capacities vary among individuals, but varying circumstances help or hinder recognition of needs and full use of capacities. Art education must not only accept these variations in interest and performance but must also sustain an atmosphere conducive to the fullest possible expression of self and the greatest possible realization of capacities. A true measure of the effectiveness of the school, the success of the teacher, and the quality of the art program is the extent to which they contribute to the student's growth now and in the immediate and distant future.
>
> A true art experience is one in which the student gives and receives in a climate where what he believes finds expression, where his expression finds organized form, and where this form brings to him a sense of the order and quality expressed in his art object.
>
> A great variety of materials and processes, the best possible equipment, and the most highly certified personnel cannot assure achievement of goals unless the goals are solidly founded on the nature of learning and growth.
>
> The scope of art experience is wide. It encompasses the likes and the dislikes of a student—his imaginings and his fears. It permits him to paint, to draw, or to model his heroes, his benefactors, even his public enemy number one. He may picture the world as he would like it, the vacation place as he would have it, his room as he would decorate it, or even himself as he would desire to be. Experiences with people, things, and situations which have impressed themselves on his memory find expression

[12] Browning, Robert. "The Ring and the Book." *The Poems of Browning.* Boston: Houghton Mifflin Co., 1895. p. 601.

in his art work, giving it the vitality of something deeply felt or vividly imagined.

Writing in this vein of thought, Van Loon recalls the story of Lao-Kung, the aged artist, who called his pupils to his deathbed and bade them rejoice as at a feast. But they, feeling that the gods had shown the artist little consideration in the material sense, were sad, and therefore, they asked their dying mentor whether his sacrifice for the sake of beauty had really been worthwhile. Indeed, they inquired whether there might be any high purpose to which a mortal might aspire.

And then:

> A strange light came into the eyes of Lao-Kung as he lifted himself from his bed. His trembling feet carried him across the room to the spot where stood one picture that he had loved best. It was a blade of grass, hastily jotted down with the strokes of his mighty brush. But the blade of grass lived and breathed. It was not merely a blade of grass, for within itself it contained the spirit of every blade of grass that had ever grown since the beginning of time.
>
> "There," the old man said, "is my answer. I have made myself the equal of the gods, for I too have touched the hem of Eternity." [13]

INDUSTRIAL AND HOME ARTS

The school that would prepare its students for the worthy use of leisure time provides opportunities for them to learn to work with tools, to understand the quality and nature of materials, and to experience the thrill of saying to themselves, "This is my handiwork." As the sculptor expresses his feelings and gets satisfaction in shaping a piece of marble, so may the artisan express himself and get satisfaction from a room or a house painted, a spigot washer replaced, a picture window draped, a garden of zinnias planted, a piece of driftwood fashioned into a work of art, a table top refinished, a chair upholstered, a rug woven, a defective motor repaired, a broken wire soldered, a fence mended, a Sunday school hall constructed, or a community speaker's platform built by volunteer hands. And he who finds and enjoys such leisure pursuits can say with Henry van Dyke, "This is my work; my blessing, not my doom." [14]

---

[13] Van Loon, Hendrik Willem. *The Arts.* New York: Simon and Schuster, 1937. p. 6.

[14] van Dyke, Henry. *Light from Many Lamps.* (Edited by Lillian Eichler Watson.) New York: Simon and Schuster, 1951. p. 136.

PHYSICAL EDUCATION

The body may not soar as high as the mind, but it can attain amazing heights. Athletes may not possess the adroitness of diplomats, but their achievements at the Olympics have won friends and influenced nations. Skill in athletics and sports requires not only a high degree of coordination but self-discipline as well.

The schools can build strong bodies for strong minds; teach good sportsmanship in the fullest sense; and foster active, happy, and satisfying leisure activities to be pursued in appropriate measure through a lifetime by providing for students, young and older—

Vigorous physical exercise

Opportunities for team participation

Swimming

Hiking

Camping

Rhythmic work and dancing.

Mozart composed for the dance. Degas painted the dance. But those who enjoy it most are those who dance. Although dancing is sometimes induced by social obligation rather than by spontaneous impulse, its vital role in daily life and in the development of cultures is universally acknowledged.

VOLUNTARY SERVICES

The most serious problem the schools are now facing is not in mastery of subject matter or in developing skills for the manipulation of concrete materials. Rather, it is to help children develop a core of values that will guide them in making decisions, in accepting responsibilities, and in forming commitments to do the very best they can in meeting obligations. The school activities program is a laboratory for developing such values and commitments. When well planned and managed, it fosters solidarity among groups of students, it identifies young people with important purposes, it aids them in establishing goals, and it absorbs their interests in purposes that transcend immediate selfish interests.

Schools today train for leadership by accenting purposeful action which will benefit the school, the home, the community, and in some measure a greater part of the world. Students learn that leadership can be maintained successfully only if one truly has a deep sense of responsibility, holds the respect of those he leads, and can count on their willing response in time of need.

In the elementary schools a child who has won the confidence and respect of his teachers and classmates is entrusted with important responsibilities. He may be selected as a representative to the student council or he may be chosen chairman of a service club. He may become the assembly leader, the yard leader, or a member of the safety patrol. The school activities program continues and expands at the secondary level. School newspapers need contributors, editors, reporters, business managers, and salesmen. Other activities, including banking programs, special interest clubs, and television programs, offer opportunities for leadership.

The school cannot impart ethical values or affect the attitudes of young people in any substantial way on a make-believe basis. At an earlier time in this country, young people of ages now in the upper grades of the secondary school would have been adults with full responsibilities for playing a useful role in community life. It is the culture and not the nature of the individual that has delayed the time for assuming such responsibilities. These young people are far too mature to get much benefit or satisfaction from make-believe activities. When ignored or treated superficially their potentials lie dormant or boil up into frustrations and resentments.

The school cannot and should not project a program that disregards or violates the mores and firmly established traditions of community life. But to the extent that it can lead young people to devote some of their leisure hours to purposeful services, it will be adding a useful dimension to their educational experiences. During recent months when the floodwaters of the Mississippi River threatened to inundate cities, towns, and villages all along its upper courses, high school students who joined adults in sandbagging the river banks demonstrated their eagerness and ability to assist in meeting an important community problem. In many instances high school students have been involved in clean-up–fix-up campaigns. They have provided useful services as volunteers in hospitals and in community drives for welfare organizations and as aides on playgrounds and in summer school programs for younger children. When young people nearing adulthood are by the very nature of society largely removed from the world of work and purposeful activities, it is imperative that teachers in planning the total educational program give serious thought to involving them during their leisure hours in useful and satisfying activities.

There can be no doubt that growth in character and ideals initiated through small beginnings in the elementary school and nurtured through the secondary school matures and bears fruit in adult life.

Many people, giving in abundance from their leisure time, serve their fellowmen through civic, welfare, cultural, and recreational enterprises. These are the men and women who play vital leadership roles in Girl Scouts and Boy Scouts, 4-H clubs, League of Women Voters, Junior Achievement, Freedoms Foundation, United Givers Fund, March of Dimes, CARE, Red Cross, Big Brothers, world affairs councils, golden age clubs, hospital aide organizations, community councils, homemaking consultant services, symphony clubs, civil defense programs, voluntary teacher aide programs, tutoring programs, and countless others.

CULTURAL WELLSPRINGS

As one looks backward in review of the wellsprings of culture to which men in all ages have turned to refresh their spirits, to broaden their visions, and to get better understanding of the meanings and purposes of life, his attention is drawn to great cities—Athens, Alexandria, Rome, Constantinople, Paris, London, Vienna, Berlin, New York, and hundreds of other cities. It is here that the wisdom gleaned from the endless efforts of people to reach their destinies in an almost infinite variety of circumstances has been reduced to comprehensible terms by sculptors, painters, musicians, novelists, historians, playwrights, scientists, and architects; it is here that this wisdom is preserved for all who would study and enjoy it in libraries, museums, and general cultural centers. Throughout all history, students, teachers, research workers, great scholars, artists, and musicians have turned to them for inspiration and guidance. Knowledge of the culture, preserved and made available in this manner, has been indispensable in guiding the course of human events. Truly these works of art and historical records have served as cultural wellsprings.

Nowadays it often seems as though the strife, turmoil, and ugliness of the city, emerging as people strive for mastery of powerful cultural forces intruding upon their lives, overshadow and obscure its cultural treasures. The drama of the unruly crowd, conflict between gangs of restless juveniles, and turmoil in the tenement districts seem to take precedence in the minds of people over the great libraries, theaters, symphonic orchestras, and art displays. At a time when the problems that confront people in all walks of life seem to be more difficult than ever before, it is doubly important that people turn to the best that is in the culture for guidance. The ills that beset mankind, in whatever form they exist, are not likely to be cured if they are ignored. But, on the other hand, repeated and ever deeper draughts of potions that cause illnesses will not cure them. Bertoldo, in commenting about one of Michelangelo's drawings which fell short of his teacher's expectations, said, "The hogshead gives the wine it contains." [15]

Unless people are sensitive to the highest ideals and values of the culture, their thoughts and actions will not be inspired and guided by them. The school, with a large measure of responsibility for nurturing and guiding the mental growth of young people, has special obligations for introducing them to the best in community life. Small communities as well as the larger ones have rich cultural resources if they are but used. Nearly every town and village has its library, its orchestra, its art display, and its cultural center. The manner and extent to which these resources are used depends upon school policy and teaching procedures.

The Philadelphia schools provide transportation during school hours and on Saturdays to take children and teachers to the Academy of Fine Arts, the Art Museum, City Orchestra concerts, the Academy of Natural Sciences, the Commercial Museum, the Franklin Institute of Science and Invention, and other centers. New York City has a comprehensive program entitled "Going Places and Seeing Things." Many other communities make provisions for group participation or urge students to take advantage of opportunities on an individual basis.

TELEVISION

Television is one of the most effective teaching devices of the times. It reaches nearly every home, and its use in the classroom is becoming common. It appeals to two-year-olds and to eighty-year-olds and all in between. There is perhaps no other pastime or activity that claims so many leisure hours as television. But there are among others, perhaps, two particularly relevant dangers in television. One is that virtually all leisure hours can be spent before the set in passive participation. The second lies in the quality of many programs. The school has a responsibility to train students, and, indirectly, adults through parent-teacher groups and other avenues, to become discriminating viewers. High standards of excellence and selectivity should be the guides.

Complaints are often made by thoughtful people that too many television programs are devoted to trivialities and are pitched at low intellectual levels. To the extent that such criticisms are well founded, the fault lies not so much in the television or with the people who plan the programs as with the tastes and expectations of the viewers. If the quality of television programs is to be improved—and there are

[15] Stone, Irving. *The Agony and the Ecstasy*. Garden City, N.Y.: Doubleday & Co., 1961. p. 68.

very few people who would contend that there is not great room for improvements—the tastes and expectations of the viewers will lead the way. It is in bringing about such changes in appreciations and wants in the total population that the school's greatest challenge in the use of television lies. Such improvements will be made, not in a revolutionary manner, but through a gradual growth process as children in the classrooms become acquainted with good productions and dissatisfied with mediocre presentations.

CONTINUING EDUCATION

The need for continuing education was never more clearly demonstrated than in 1960 when millions of people sat down in the quiet of their homes to listen to the Kennedy-Nixon debates on the great issues before the country at that time. This discussion clearly showed that the issues submitted to the voters for decision are becoming increasingly complex. As simpler problems have been resolved or have receded into positions of less consequence, they have been replaced with issues that are less clear-cut and that call for greater understanding and keener powers of reasoning. These problems—political, social, intellectual, and vocational—encompass the entire cultural spectrum. Whatever they are and however they are cast, they constitute the content of a lifelong educational program.

Fortunately, time for mastery of these problems increases as the time required to earn a living steadily diminishes. Even during middle life, when most persons have full employment and are striving for advancement in their occupational fields or for improvement in their economic position, there is time available for education. School systems are providing opportunities for using this leisure time for worthy purposes through accredited evening high schools where people from 17 to 77 can pursue courses commonly offered in the high school as well as classes on the elementary level. Many school systems offer a wide variety of programs relating to leisure time pursuits, to appreciation of the arts, and to building physical fitness. In day and evening vocational schools, supported in large measure by federal funds, men and women displaced by automation and changing manpower needs are retrained for employment. The American Association of School Administrators, through resolutions adopted at the 1965 convention, urged administrators in state and local school systems to take vigorous leadership in developing and maintaining an educational program to provide appropriate education from kindergarten through at least two years beyond high school and continuing education for all adults.

In many communities senior citizens meet in public day and evening schools to study problems of retirement, arts and crafts, typing, English, current events, dramatics, and other fields. Some localities are experimenting with community centers where golden age clubs and recreational and civic groups meet.

SOMETHING TO DO

In "The Secret of Happiness Is Something To Do," the author tells of the poet, John Burroughs:

> The poet stood at his window and watched a neighbor walk by. He walked—not as a man should, in joy and triumph—but with slow step and sagging shoulders, like a man with a great burden on his soul.
>
> John Burroughs knew why. The man had no work he loved, nothing to keep him busy and content, to give his days purpose and direction.[16]

Burroughs had once experienced this unhappiness. Later he took his pen and wrote an essay that has been quoted many times. Here are the closing paragraphs:

> What is the best thing for a stream? It is to keep moving. If it stops, it stagnates. So the best thing for a man is that which keeps the currents going—the physical, the moral, and the intellectual currents. Hence the secret of happiness is—something to do; some congenial work. Take away the occupation of all men, and what a wretched world it would be!
>
> Few persons realize how much of their happiness is dependent upon their work, upon the fact that they are kept busy and not left to feed upon themselves. Happiness comes most to persons who seek her least, and think least about it. It is not an object to be sought; it is a state to be induced. It must follow and not lead. It must overtake you, and not you overtake it. How important is health to happiness, yet the best promoter of health is *something to do.*
>
> Blessed is the man who has some congenial work, some occupation in which he can put his heart, and which affords a complete outlet to all the forces there are in him.[17]

Incidentally, it should be noted in the above illustration that Burroughs was standing by his window, thinking. The good teacher often reminds his students that there is another mile on the road to happiness. It's called, "time to speculate, to dream, to meditate."

---

[16] Watson, Lillian Eichler, editor. *Light from Many Lamps.* New York: Simon and Schuster, 1951. p. 3.

[17] Burroughs, John. *Light from Many Lamps.* (Edited by Lillian Eichler Watson.) New York: Simon and Schuster, 1951. p. 5.

IMPERATIVE

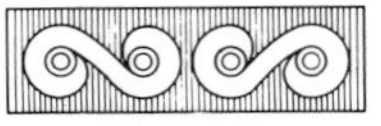

10 · TO WORK WITH OTHER PEOPLES OF THE WORLD FOR HUMAN BETTERMENT

Distributed over the earth are 3 billion people—men, women, and children. They live in great cities, in small towns and country villages, on rich farmlands, in tropical jungles, along the edges of barren deserts, in high mountain valleys, along the shores of the oceans, and on the wide sweeps of the Arctic tundra. They are seamen, traders, herdsmen, industrial workers, and tillers of the soil. They speak many different languages and the differences in their cultural backgrounds are almost infinite.

> [They] eat everything from walrus blubber to crepe suzettes, live in everything from caves to skyscrapers, and wear everything from simple dhotis or loincloths to luxurious saris and Paris gowns. They travel by snowshoe, foot, cart, train, and airplane. They communicate in an infinite variety of ways, from drums to radio and television. Their occupations can be numbered by the hundreds, ranging from the farmers who use sticks to plow their fields to the people who watch over the robot machines in ultramodern factories.[1]

Yet in today's world, all are neighbors and interdependent. Events in a chain of islands in the South Pacific, in a Siberian village, in a South American city, or on the delta of the Nile are quickly known all over the world and may have profound influence in shaping the course of history and determining the future life of an Iowa farm boy whose immediate concern is increasing the yield of corn and raising better pigs.

---

[1] Kenworthy, Leonard S. *Introducing Children to the World.* New York: Harper & Brothers, 1956. p. 77.

Revolutionary changes in communication and transportation and increased interdependence have brought all peoples of the world closer together and made men of all races, creeds, and cultural backgrounds neighbors. But these cultural changes have fallen short of making neighbors live comfortably with each other. As everyone knows, not all neighbors are good neighbors. Rubbing elbows sometimes creates friction, and lack of understanding often leads to suspicion, distrust, and uneasiness. A physical world neighborhood of men has been created, but a psychological neighborhood based on common moral principles and mutual confidence and respect is yet to be realized. One who views the realities of life with clear discernment cannot but see that the interests of well-intentioned and high-minded people are sometimes in conflict. Some wants can be satisfied only at the expense of others—two hungers cannot be appeased by the same bread.

With wider dissemination of information, new hopes have been kindled, new wants have been created, and new problems have emerged. Millions of people in countries where the culture had been static for centuries are now asserting themselves in the world neighborhood. Millions whose voices were never before heard are demanding better standards of living, equality of opportunity, and a greater measure of political freedom.

> Since 1947 no fewer than 46 self-governing nations have come into being. Their citizens, numbering close to half the human race, are acutely conscious of other gnawing wants besides food, shelter, and clothing. They want to be accepted as equals in dignity. They want us to get their slants on life, discover their ancient cultures, appreciate their modern aspirations.[2]

With rapid rise of expectancies, people in these new nations look to the United States for leadership and expect assistance in their strivings. They are haunted by the fears of poverty, war, and subjugation. Their immediate needs are food, medicine, technical assistance, and educational leadership.

People in many parts of the world—Africa, Asia, Latin America, Oceania—are attempting to move rapidly from a simple or even primitive way of life into a technological culture that has been centuries in developing in Western nations. They are impatient, and the forces of progress are exceedingly slow. Their impatience often mounts to tensions; these tensions are transmitted into national pressures and often into revolutionary movements that threaten to erupt into violence of national or even international consequence.

---

[2] U.S. National Commission for UNESCO. *Mind Your World.* Washington, D.C.: Government Printing Office, 1964. p. 4.

CULTURAL CONFLICT

The tragedy of this cultural conflict is evident in several ways. First, it is evident in various forms of arrogance. Arrogance rarely arises from confidence in one's own condition but usually springs from a belief in the superiority of a chosen loyalty, whether it be to a king, to a community, or to a culture. Most great conflicts are not between men, but between ideas and organizations with which men identify themselves. It is paradoxical, therefore, that the cultures that adopt such labels as "Christian," "Western," or "humanist" should continue to pursue their controversies with such vigor and such venom. Cultural conflict appears to be the illicit offspring of institutionalized arrogance.

Second, there is cultural intolerance, with its resistance to understanding and reason. Many examples of such intolerance could be cited. It is not unknown in the United States or in any other part of the world. The ancient and modern conflict between Israel and Islam is but one example. Intolerance of the ideas of various religious groups and races is the cause of unrest in great segments of Asia and Africa. Wherever it is found, cultural intolerance restrains freedom and retards progress toward human betterment.

A third kind of tragedy exists where only the cultural patterns of the past guide visions of the future. All cultures have elaborate mechanisms for preserving and reconstructing the past. Occasionally a past has been reconstructed that is more glowing than ever existed. To refer to this as a tragedy is preposterous unless it is recognized that the people of almost every nation are rather firmly convinced that they are better than anyone else. If a nation conquers another nation, the conquering people tend to look condescendingly on those they have conquered. The victor writes the history of the battle. In his record he often places both rightness and righteousness on the side of the victor. He claims cultural as well as military superiority, and there is the added implication that this superiority will be permanent.

There is little historical evidence of permanent cultural superiority, nor is there any current evidence that any nation or culture is better or worse than others in any important way; under optimum conditions each can make a significant contribution to the material and the intellectual well-being of mankind. But in efforts to preserve a cultural past, historians and teachers often obscure the richness in other cultures by surrounding themselves with an outer shell of cultural superiority. This shell, worn to keep their pride from being wounded, acts as a barrier to recognition of values in other cultures.

THE NEW ROLE OF EDUCATION

The historical antecedents of cultural conflict are numerous. Use of education in resolving problems of cultural conflict is a modern experiment. If education succeeds in this experiment, it will be because education has come to occupy a new role in all countries.

Until recent decades education was considered more a property right than a human right. Like other property rights it was held mainly by the elite or the rich or both. Like other forms of wealth, education widens the area of choice available to an individual and increases the feasibility of the alternatives chosen. This has always been an advantage available to the rich and envied universally by the poor. To have a wide area of choice is something everyone wants, and the narrowness of choice is the degrading element of poverty. Choice not only gives pleasure; it is also an essential element of human dignity.

In recent years there has been worldwide recognition that education is a human right, an essential element of human dignity, and an imperative in the process of development in every country. Many poor countries have envied rich countries in the same way that poor people have envied rich people. Poor countries are now beginning to rely on education to increase their range and feasibility of choice. It has been almost universally accepted as the best means for developing the potential of individuals and nations. Education has become the central affirmative force in the world.

In its new role education has developed utilitarian qualities; its immediate concern is helping people acquire the understanding and the skills needed to cope with the problems immediately before them, whether they be in the field of health, nutrition, economic production, family life, or self-government. No part of the world today can claim to have the traditional, classical, elite-centered education of a century ago. In all countries education has become increasingly practical, and in many countries, more secular. Discussions of education or educational problems have preoccupied almost every world forum of peace or of planning.

Education did not always have parity of esteem with other national or international goals, and there is no assurance that it will continue to have such priority. Viewed as a form of wealth, as an element of human dignity, and as a means of development, education is not merely an axiomatic response to a worldwide need. It is a modern experiment in improving the quality of the human family. It is central to the hopes and expectations of people throughout all countries in the world.

AN INTELLECTUAL BASIS FOR COOPERATION

International understanding is based on wisdom, mutual respect, search for truth, and reduction of dogma. An intellectual basis for cooperation is needed to accommodate both the thresholds of change and the confluence of cultures.

The thresholds of change are only partly visible. The move from an agricultural to an industrial economy is now history in the developed countries. The move from rural to urban living has now occurred in most countries irrespective of their level of development. The move from a natural to a man-made environment is a subtle change which still defies analysis.

All of these changes were prompted by exploding technology. As technological advance occurred, populations began to increase faster and people began to travel and to communicate more freely and, in general, to rely more on one another. This interdependence is not a planned element of technological change; it is a by-product of change. Even man-made environment is largely the unintended result of what men do rather than a result of their planned efforts.

Technological change began in a world that was both underoccupied and underdeveloped. Thus, it was possible for the technological explosion to race forward without encountering limitations inherent in man-made environments. For centuries the population of the Western world remained relatively stable, but during the past 100 years it has almost tripled. This phenomenal increase has created a huge working population in the United States and in Western Europe. While automation of the textile industry 150 years ago could and did move the weavers from the hearths in their cottages to the factories in the towns and cities, the number of people involved was relatively small and the movement slow. Now technological inventions which are coming to the forefront in the industrial world may, if not controlled, cause real displacement in the labor force. Machines have been created that have relieved men from backbreaking drudgery in many fields of production, but unemployment problems have accompanied these great improvements.

The problems of a technological age are not solely or even largely technological. They are cultural, political, and educational. As humans become more interdependent and as they rely more on man-made environments, there is need to question the international consequences of technological change. Political institutions and cultural attitudes are hard pressed to accommodate an accelerating rate of technological change at a time when population is rapidly increasing and becoming more interdependent and possibly more intolerant.

Economic and technical cooperation is now a reality at higher levels of government. An intellectual basis of cooperation is a goal yet to be achieved, with education leading the way toward better understanding of cultural differences.

As the customs, mores, traditions, artifacts, values, and institutions of different cultures converge and intermingle in a worldwide community, the need for an intellectual basis of cooperation increases. Cultural streams are often identified by misleading labels. "The East" or "the Far East" are labels used by people from the West to identify Asiatic cultures. Non-Westerners do not use them to identify themselves. Members of non-Western cultures have long been handicapped by having their cultures interpreted to the West by Westerners. Histories of Africa, for example, are not written from an African point of view. The African who would read the history of his own continent must often read an account written by an expatriate with a Western point of view.

Westernization and its historical antecedent, the Age of Discovery, had an overpowering effect on the world. The Age of Reason, also in the context of Western history, had similar effects. These were extensions of the Judeo-Christian culture on a global scale. Into this culture stream new and important tributaries from Asia, the Orient, Africa, and Latin America are flowing. These tributaries are changing the character of the mainstream by introducing new loyalties and new values.

Educational programs in non-Western cultures give a great deal of attention to the West. Western, and particularly American, educational programs have given but little attention to the non-West. Yet cultures from the East and, indeed, from every part of the world are commingling in a world community and exerting a profound influence on intellectual progress. *It is imperative that programs of study in the elementary and secondary schools of this country be revised and procedures of instruction be improved so that children can become more familiar with the rich traditions of the civilizations of the Middle East, of the Far East, and of the newly emerging nations in Africa.*

GRASPING VALUES

When the American student examines values of other cultures, he finds that they show many of the same hopes, fears, sympathies, and prejudices that he has.

Getting a grasp of values is no easy task. Even within a single culture, it is difficult to recognize that middle class values are different from lower class values. A school oriented to the middle class encounters difficulties in motivating and in educating students from lower classes. The social distance between subcultures is difficult to comprehend. Except when examined as curiosities or oddities, the values of different cultures are even more difficult to understand. It is necessary, nevertheless, if international understanding is to be realized and if the schools accept this responsibility.

Values are the constructs of cultures, and cultures are streams of ideas, beliefs, customs, and perhaps material objects. All of man's effort and all of man's creative behavior is relevant to his values.

Viewed at one extreme in this context, man is simply a creature of his culture and can exercise no control over it. He may have hopes, plans, and aspirations, but these are subordinate and in the long run they are not effective in cultural change. Culture is the cause, according to this view, and man's behavior is the result. Even race prejudice, attitudes toward thrift, and acceptance of religion are to be explained as manifestations of culture itself and not as individual values giving shape to culture. Humans are merely the carriers of culture, the instruments through which culture expresses itself, and the dependent variables of the culture's value system. This view of culture is an appealing one. It is impersonal; it does not require the study of man as an individual; and yet it provides explanations of his behavior.

At the other extreme is the view that man can exercise some control over his destiny. His goals, aspirations, and plans are of prime importance, and his culture is the consequence rather than the cause of his behavior. Man in his search for dignity is not only the carrier of culture but the creator of it. Viewed in this context, man is the independent variable and his culture is dependent.

Neither of these extreme views is completely acceptable. Education is more than a reflection of society, a trade-school for learning the values of immutable schemes, or the process of adjusting to preestablished norms. Individual differences are important, values are learned, and differences in individual values are a part of the reality of the educational environment. Similarly, cultural differences are important, cultural values are learned within a cultural context, and a study of these differences may be an important way to examine one's own culture as well as other cultures.

The minimum reward for studying other cultures of the world and working with people from other lands may be recognition and appreciation of nobleness in all lands and in all cultures. The optimum reward may be recognition that the strength of society depends on the margin it allows for interpretations by others. How a culture makes accommodations within its own sphere is its own business, but accommodation with other cultures is the price that it must pay to live in society.

There is a remarkable opportunity to reexamine one's own cultural values through study of other cultures. This should not be regarded as merely a fringe benefit of cross-cultural study; it may be justified as a main purpose. As education becomes more secular, it is increasingly difficult to deal with the value orientations of students. Moreover, there is resistance to questioning values which have deep and abiding meaning to the individual and to the nation as a whole. Ways must be found to teach children how to respect deep-seated values and customs of other people without losing or diminishing in any degree their confidence, respect, and commitment to the ideals, values, and customs of their own culture. Everyone must clearly understand that there is nothing incompatible between love of one's own country and respect for the values and virtues of people of other lands.

UNIVERSAL PROBLEMS AND NEEDS

There are common barriers to the study of other lands and other cultures. Although not insurmountable, these barriers are difficult to recognize and to understand. The most obvious barrier is language. Invariably, language carries a cultural and political bias. It determines what literature will be read and what communications systems will develop. It establishes a framework for the accumulation of knowledge. The importance of language differences to world understanding has often been underestimated. Language differences restrict the interchange of cultural understanding.

Geographical distance is another cultural barrier. Modern transportation has closed the time gap of distance, but distance is still a fact to be reckoned with. Even though almost unbelievable strides have been taken in improving the means and ease of travel, the overwhelming majority of students and teachers are still confined by the barriers of distance and must rely on books, newspapers, films, artifacts, ideas, and chance meetings with people who have visited other lands to give them an understanding of other cultures.

The complexities of international trade are additional barriers to understanding other cultures. Trade is a well established fact of international life but is conducted through complex systems of agreements, tariffs, customs, duties, taxes, quotas, and standards. These regulations apply in different ways to different countries. Most countries, however, have special provisions to encourage the exchange of printed materials.

There may be other barriers to the study of other cultures, including the difficulty of understanding the time-frames of technical and social developments. In the United States, for example, the time-frame for the universal adoption of television was about ten years, while the time-frame for full recognition and acceptance of civil rights for Negroes has been more than one hundred years. In other countries the time-frame for the adoption of television may be close to one hundred years, while the extension of civil rights to all citizens may take less than ten years.

It should be emphasized that barriers to the study of other cultures are not necessarily insurmountable obstacles. In fact, they can intensify interest and become focal points of attention. Common elements overtly expressed in every culture can also become focal points of interest and study. Almost every country, for example, has accepted the *Declaration of Human Rights,* developed by nations working together in the United Nations. Its interpretation may be different in different cultures, but its principles have been accepted as a recognition of the common rights of all people. Education also has been accepted as an essential by all countries and is considered by most countries an important aspect of international cooperation. UNESCO was established to promote international cooperation in education.

INTERNATIONAL EDUCATION

The current widespread interest in international education and the study of other cultures is not a transient phenomenon. It is a permanent upwelling of human will in search of human dignity. It is based on humanitarianism. It is motivated by search for national security and an extension of freedom. It is not sufficient to identify international education and to describe it with righteous and irrelevant platitudes and devotional rhetoric. It is the most contemporary element of the current international scene. Every elementary and secondary age student will be affected by the accomplishments and failures of international education.

Colleges and universities are becoming extensively involved in international education, but these efforts should be extended. In urgent language directed at colleges, graduate schools, and their constituents, a recent report had this to say:

> . . . what is most needed is . . . a clear and unequivocal institutional commitment to what in shorthand fashion we have called the international studies dimension of liberal education. It is too late merely to play with new ideas. The changes which are now called for cannot be accomplished in a halfhearted way. They require recogni-

> tion on the part of both faculty and students that the new international dimension is not an extra, but an integral part of the educational program.[3]

The problem of organizing a program of instruction in international education at the college and university level is comparable in at least one respect to the problem of organizing such a program at the elementary and secondary school level. There is no natural or convenient niche or category in which one may place international studies. Present subjects or disciplines are not inappropriate, but neither are they organized to give students a meaningful acquaintance with cultures other than their own. When present disciplines were created, they emerged as accidents or in response to the needs of society. Creative forces operating at the time did not reflect the full need for intercultural education.

A subject is only a scholar's way of describing a segment of world reality. A subject is merely a useful form of organization for teaching and learning knowledge which already exists. Wherever and whenever reorganization of curriculum content or the introduction of new courses is necessary to international education, such changes should be made. The reordering of their curriculums to give adequate attention to world affairs is a task that still confronts most colleges and universities.

> Such pioneering efforts as the oriental civilizations program at Columbia, the programs on Chinese, Indian and Arab civilizations at Chicago, the Asian survey courses at such places as California (Berkeley) and Michigan, and other approaches at Indiana, Arizona, and elsewhere deserve careful study by universities and colleges that have yet to take similar steps.[4]

In the meantime, in most institutions of higher education, such general courses as "World History" and "World Civilization" provide the best available opportunities to develop the undergraduate student's international perspective. Courses in such fields as government, economics, history, and sociology also provide opportunities for developing understanding of international affairs.

ELEMENTARY AND SECONDARY SCHOOLS

The problem of organizing the curriculum for international studies is even more challenging at the elementary and secondary school level.

---

[3] Committee on the College and World Affairs. *The College and World Affairs*. New York: Education and World Affairs, 1964. p. 67.

[4] Committee on the University and World Affairs. *The University and World Affairs*. New York: Ford Foundation, 1960. pp. 17-18.

It is also more important. By far the greatest accomplishment in understanding other peoples of the world will be made through the public elementary and secondary schools. These schools more nearly reach all the people than any other institution or operational program. It is because of their almost universal coverage and their orientation to the development of reason and understanding that the opportunity of the schools to contribute to maintaining peaceful relationships among the nations of the world is so great.

Many promising programs are under way. Some states have established a "world cultures" course as a requirement. "World affairs" is emphasized in extracurricular programs, units on cultures of the world are being introduced into the social studies program, and teachers workshops and institutes on international education are held with more frequency. These and other developments throughout the elementary and secondary program clearly show that teachers, administrators, and the general public as well are recognizing the importance of international education.

The task of helping nearly 200 million Americans become internationally oriented—become more familiar with the hopes and aspirations, the wants and needs, and the beliefs and values of other peoples of the world—is no small undertaking. Programs at the elementary and secondary school level will be most effective, for they reach virtually everyone. Speaking at the November 1965 White House Conference on Education, Robb said:

> The whole process starts with little children. We must be concerned not only with bright, eager children, but with the unfolding minds of the average and the not-so-bright child and the child whose cultural base is largely one of disadvantage. These children are numerous and they perceive the world in a different way from our version and our vision of it—and this limits their perspectives. We need to involve the American school—both public and private—in ways and in depth never before undertaken in world affairs.[5]

There is danger that the problem will appear too complicated, too difficult, and too remote. Some teachers and administrators and some lay citizens think of international education in the grandiose proportions of world citizenship and world society, in terms that almost eliminate cultural lines. Such thinking is unrealistic. Recognition that cultural differences do exist, that various forms of social organization do exist and will continue to exist, and that different forms of government will prevail is one of the most effective ways of easing tensions and reducing frictions among people.

---

[5] Robb, Felix C. "Education of Americans for International Cooperation." Address to White House Conference on Education, Washington, D. C., November 30, 1965. (From mimeographed copy of speech.)

In all of these efforts, it is imperative that the emphasis be on educating for world understanding. Understanding is basic to the acceptance of other people, whether they are similar or different. When children in the classroom learn this important principle, it will help them develop ability to work with rather than against other people. The concept of world understanding is broad and all-encompassing and has many dimensions. Before teachers and students can work effectively on this important problem, it has to be broken down into segments of manageable size. In a pilot program developed cooperatively by the National Council for the Social Studies and the Glens Falls, New York, school system, the instructional program was organized around four primary goals:

> (1) *Increasing* understanding of world affairs; (2) *developing* an appreciation of other peoples and cultures; (3) *inculcating* an attitude of respect toward foreign peoples; and (4) *promoting* a sense of responsibility for furthering better understanding of foreign peoples and cultures.[6]

The program of international education developed in this school system provided a wide variety of activities and experiences adapted to the different age levels and abilities of pupils in the school. Most teaching activities were carefully planned as a part of the regular school program, but some were carried on as extracurricular activities, culminating in assembly programs. To illustrate, pupils in a first-grade class invited a teacher from Japan to visit their classroom. After this visiting teacher had answered many questions about life in Japan, he taught a lesson in paper folding to show how children in the Japanese schools made birds and other likenesses from paper. Because their interest was aroused, children brought from their homes to the classroom postcards, stamps, toys, dolls, articles of clothing, dishes, chopsticks, and other artifacts of Japanese life. Through such filmstrips as *Togo and Muki of Japan, Japan: Country Life,* and *Japan: Our School Life,* the children learned similarities and differences between American and Japanese ways of living. In a third-grade class in the same school, the children developed a tape recording of a classroom program and exchanged it with a third-grade class in a Japanese school.

A fifth-grade teacher in one of the Glens Falls schools developed programs of folk dances.

> One of these programs developed into an assembly program which included folk dances from several countries. "The Virginia Reel"

[6] Long, Harold M., and King, Robert N. *Improving the Teaching of World Affairs: The Glens Falls Story*. Washington, D.C.: National Council for the Social Studies, 1964. p. 46.

was used to represent the United States. Mexico was interpreted through the "Hat Dance." Using *Fun Around the World* (Women's Guild of the United Nations), the class found information to create a scene on Judica, a Czech holiday, which provided an opportunity to dance "The Wheat." The Danish dance, "The Seven Jumps," was related to a pre-Lenten celebration of Shrove Tuesday. A Hebrew calendar provided information about the Israeli "Hora," a dance associated with the theme of Israel's independence day in May. Costumes were kept simple. Decorations, including flags, were authentic.[7]

In a fifth-grade classroom in the Edgewood School in Scarsdale, New York, a Japanese house was built to scale under the direction of a boy born in Japan. When the house was completed, the boy's mother came to the school to teach flower arrangements to the pupils. In a study of Indonesia in a junior high school in Scarsdale, a question came up about the size of Indonesian houses which books did not answer. An enterprising boy in this class found pictures of Indonesian homes in old copies of the *National Geographic*. From these pictures, he estimated the size of the houses from the figures of men and women in the pictures and made models of the homes.

These examples illustrate how the creative energies of pupils in the classroom can be directed toward gaining better understanding of the cultures of other peoples of the world if their imaginations are kindled and they are given opportunity.

Activities for the sake of activity have but little meaning; they must be related to the development of concepts that will help children now and in the years to come organize their thinking about other cultures. At the upper elementary grade level and in the junior high school, children are able to grasp the basic ideas that—

There are many countries and cultures in the world, some large, some small, some new, some old, but all important. Each country and culture does something especially well. Some take care of old people well; some take better care of children; some concentrate on the arts; some specialize in science.

Countries and cultures are constantly changing. In the period of exploration, for example, China and India were great, dominant, and well developed nations; but for long periods their cultures were relatively dormant. Today these cultures are undergoing important changes and coming to the forefront as great powers.

Some countries and cultures are more adaptable than others. The United States and Japan, for example, are countries that have

---

[7] *Ibid.*, pp. 50-51.

learned new ways of living quickly. Other countries have resisted change and have been slow to adapt to new circumstances.

Peoples of all countries are proud of their cultures. It is difficult for young children and even for many adults to realize that the people of other countries are as proud of their cultures as the people of the United States are of their culture.

There are great variations within countries and cultures. Through oversimplification, people frequently refer to "the French point of view," "the Asiatic mind," "the Latin American temperament," or "the British sense of humor." Such stereotypes, when used, tend to close one's mind to the richness and the multitude of variations in any culture.

Cultures are affected by many factors. Climate, vegetation, nearness to the sea, rivers and mountains, and presence or absence of mineral deposits affect the cultures of countries.

Small countries as well as large countries are important. People in the United States tend, because of the size of this nation, to emphasize bigness and to minimize the importance of small nations. Children and, indeed, everybody should become more fully aware that some of the most important problems on the world scene develop in small countries and some of the most important contributions to the cultures of the world have come from smaller countries.

Complete understanding of a country or a culture is almost impossible. To place this problem in perspective, one needs only to help children visualize how difficult it would be for even the most discerning visitor from another country to understand fully the culture of the United States. This difficulty should not prevent a student from undertaking studies of other countries, but calling attention to the problem may develop an appropriate sense of humility as one approaches the important task of learning to know other peoples of the world.[8]

The program in international education at the senior high school level may be as wide and as varied as the curriculum. Each department will find opportunities to enrich and improve instruction by developing a world affairs viewpoint. To illustrate: students in some schools—

Read English language editions of newspapers or magazines published in such other countries as Canada, the United Kingdom, India, and Pakistan.

---

[8] Acknowledgment is expressed to Kenworthy, Leonard S., *op. cit.*, pp. 134-37.

Compare the views of scientists and statesmen from different countries on such issues as disarmament, public health, and population growth.

Listen to recordings of music indigenous to the cultures of different countries.

Share in the school's efforts to entertain overseas guests in homes and in the community.

Visit the United Nations headquarters as an organized student group.

List American authors to be recommended to overseas students.

Recommend books on world affairs for purchase by the school library.

Arrange to show prints or slides of art from various countries.

There is no one best way to help students learn about the cultures of other lands. They learn in various ways, and different facets of the culture lend themselves to different media of instruction. Some students learn about other cultures from people; some through books, films, radio, and television; and some through hobbies such as stamp or coin collecting.

Intercultural values and international problems must come alive through all of the devices that can be employed. Foreign visitors, exchange teachers, and special programs are especially valuable. Most important is the realization that members of other cultures, their problems, and their values are tangible and relevant to similar problems in our own culture.

It is imperative that schools all over this country give greater effort than has ever been given before to helping young people become familiar with the cultures of other peoples of the world and learn how to work with them in a fruitful manner toward the accomplishment of broad common purposes—maintenance of peace, elimination of famine, treatment and control of disease, recognition of basic human rights, desalinization of sea water, exploration of outer space and the depths of the sea—and in sharing literary, musical, and artistic productions. It is all-important that young people learn how to be at home in the world.

> Ahead of them lies the gigantic, but infinitely rewarding, task of learning to know and understand other peoples, and the equally difficult task of helping other peoples to know and understand them.[9]

---

[9] Roosevelt, Eleanor. *Tomorrow Is Now.* First Perennial Library edition. New York: Harper and Row, 1964. p. 86.

If the people of this country would have their children grow up to respect all men and to seek for others the same opportunities that they desire for themselves, it is imperative that the schools help children develop those skills, understandings, and attitudes needed by people of all nations to live together in peace and goodwill.

IMPERATIVE

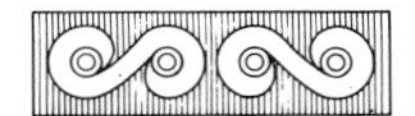

11 · IN MEETING THE NEEDS OF ALL PEOPLE

Ever since the days of the Latin grammar school and the dame school in early colonial life, the people of this country have from time to time redefined their educational goals. Forces operating in the culture at a particular period and educational needs arising from these forces have been the basis for this redefinition.

In times of rapid cultural transition when the lives of people have been shaken and unsettled by dramatic changes in industrial enterprise, rapid population growth, marked movement of great groups of people from one part of the country to another, far-reaching scientific discoveries, the opening of new frontiers, and extensive military involvement, concerted attempts have been made to reshape educational goals. In times of stress these efforts have been marked by tensions among people; by anxieties; by attacks on what the schools are doing and not doing; and by criticism of educational philosophy, expenditures, and basic educational purposes. Through experimentation, research, and sober thought on the part of forward-looking people, the force of these tensions has been directed toward constructive ends and educational goals have been reshaped and redefined with a posture a little higher on the scale of human endeavor. This assessment of circumstances, identification of needs, and redefinition of educational goals has been a part of the whole process of cultural advancement in this country.

It may not be out of place to call attention here to a few well known circumstances in which educational goals in this country have been defined and redefined. In the early colonial period when people were striving for independence, grasping for freedom, and reaching for a destiny that they believed to be in keeping with the dignity of the human spirit, they were guided by religious and philosophical concepts. Formal schooling had but little relationship to the business of earning a living. The skills and knowledge that people needed to build homes, to provide food and clothing for their families, and to carry on the affairs of community life could be learned for the most part through actual experience as sons worked with their fathers in the clearings and daughters aided their mothers in household tasks. The concepts of the freedom and independence they sought were couched in the philosophy of Calvin, Luther, Hobbes, and Locke. The languages of the scholars were Greek, Latin, and Hebrew. Church leaders were the disseminators of information and thought. Consequently, the educational goals that emerged in early colonial life emphasized reading the Scriptures and learning Latin and Greek. Such goals and the educational program which supported them would be totally out of place in today's culture but were perhaps adequate for that frontier age.

But in the dynamic culture emerging on this new continent, circumstances changed. Commerce began to grow. Ships from different countries began carrying on vigorous trade with the West Indies and Europe. Small settlements along the Eastern seaboard emerged into cities, and business transactions began to claim a major place in the culture. At this time, Benjamin Franklin took the leadership in redefining goals of education. When he founded the Academy at Philadelphia, he emphasized the importance of navigation, bookkeeping, accounting, geography, and arithmetic. He and those who worked with him in redefining educational goals saw that the study of these new cultural developments was more important to the well-being of individuals and to community life than the study of Latin, Greek, and Hebrew. Attention in the schools he proposed was focused mainly on problems people encountered in daily living. Following this redefinition of goals, which gained considerable acceptance, academies sprang up all over the country. In response to this redefinition of educational goals, the character of the educational program and the character of the schools changed.

Again, in the period immediately following World War I, when President Wilson's Fourteen Points and the League of Nations were being debated around the world, the people of this country turned their attention to reshaping educational goals. Prior to this period, completion of an elementary education was generally held to be reasonable preparation for effective citizenship. But within the few years between 1914 and 1920, horizons broadened and industry expanded to the point that the problems and issues confronting the people at the voting booths, in town meetings, in city councils, and in legislative assemblies had become so complex that minimum preparation for effective citizenship had to be extended to the high school level. It was at this time that the Seven Cardinal Principles gained wide acceptance as broad educational goals. They reflected concern about community life, state and national government, international relationships, an increasingly complex business and industrial enterprise, ethical and spiritual values, physical health and well-being, and the aesthetic elements of the culture. This redefinition of goals at a time when the country began to be recognized as one of the leading world powers and to assume a role of leadership in world affairs laid the foundation for the comprehensive high school.

During the decade of the thirties, when the nation was shaken to its very roots by the Great Depression and attention was focused on the needs of people whose lives had been disrupted through a cultural upheaval that no one seemed to clearly understand, the people of this country once again moved to reshape and redefine their educational goals. The Educational Policies Commission accepted the challenge to digest from the fermenting forces that permeated every segment of the culture a statement of the hopes and aspirations of people for an educational program. These goals were stated as—

Self realization

Human relationship

Economic efficiency

Civic responsibility.

As these goals were set and programs in the schools were modified in keeping with these general directives, attention was focused sharply on the needs of people as individuals and the relationship of these needs to the well-being of the nation as a whole. Nursery schools were established, and the practice of giving physical examinations to children in the schools emerged. Schools gave more attention to health, nutrition, and dental care, and school lunch programs were initiated. Millions of young men who had nothing to do and no place to go were enrolled in the CCC program. School district reorganization that would provide better educational opportunities for millions of children got under way. The length of the school term, particularly in rural areas, was extended from 5 or 6 months to 9 months. Teacher preparation was strengthened, and people began to pin greater hopes on education than they ever had before.

Now we are in another period when great cultural changes are taking place. This is a period in which a technological society calls for more research, more creative thought and action, broader and deeper knowledge of the sciences, more highly developed mathematical skills, more highly skilled workers, and greater understanding of the culture of other nations than ever before. It is a period when the defense needs of the country call for men and women who are alert, responsible, and informed. It is a period in which international relations have broadened, with dimensions far greater and more extensive than one could have dreamed of a generation ago. It is a period when rural and urban cultures are clashing and underprivileged people everywhere are reaching upward for rights and recognition they believe to be theirs. It is a period in which outer space challenges the imagination, the creativity, and the technical skills of a whole generation of people. It is a period of instantaneous communication, of almost unbelievable speed of travel, and of physical energy almost too great to be comprehended. These forces are playing upon the schools and generating new and different educational needs. They are making people uneasy about education and moving them to redefine educational goals.

Here are some of the upward thrusts, contentions, and expressions of beliefs that come from people who view educational needs and the purposes of the school from different vantage points—

> Some people believe that educational goals should be set in terms of higher academic standards, that requirements for graduation from high school should be higher and more stringent, and that students should have more homework.
>
> Some people who are disturbed by the uncertainties of the times and are searching for something permanent to hold to seem to want to return to the "good old days" of a rigidly defined, closely knit, highly disciplined curriculum.
>
> Some people see advantages in adapting methods of mass production to teaching and learning. There is so much to learn that is important and this country has had such successful experience with mass production methods in industry that it seems only reasonable that schools could borrow practices from this industrial experience and use them to good advantage in reshaping the instructional program.
>
> Some people who see the future of mankind depending in large part upon research and scientific development want greater objectivity in the instructional program.

Some people who are greatly concerned about physical fitness want physical education programs strengthened.

Some people whose lives are intricately related to business and industry want an educational program that will supply the technical skills and know-how needed to keep enterprise operating at an ever-increasing level of productivity.

Some people who are sensitive to occupational opportunities and requirements in the labor force see need for reshaping the vocational education programs in the schools to bring them up-to-date with the needs and demands of a new age.

Some college administrators who are swamped with increasing enrollments and pressed with demands for reliable and capable people insist on tougher admission standards and a more rigorous program of college work.

Some people in the fields of modern languages and international relationships insist on more emphasis on foreign languages in the instructional program.

Some officials in the federal government and leaders of great foundations, in their zeal to improve instruction, are reaching out by various means to put more strength in the teaching of mathematics, science, English, and foreign languages.

Some people in the field of mental health who are deeply concerned about the psychological tensions that engulf many children, youth, and adults in this changing society want more psychological services and better counseling programs.

Some behavioral scientists who, through research and experimentation, have gained new insights into the forces that affect human behavior want the schools to give more attention to group behavior and environmental circumstances.

Some people who are deeply aware of the rich cultural heritage that has been recorded and transmitted from one generation to another through literature, music, paintings, and sculpture want greater emphasis given to the humanities and the fine arts.

Some people who are troubled about the moral stamina of society insist that greater attention be given to the development of moral and spiritual values.

Some people who see the challenges of self-government becoming more complex and trying want the schools to place more emphasis on the principles and processes of democracy.

Some people who see a great reservoir of potential for human betterment lying dormant and unused as work days and work weeks become shorter emphasize the need for teaching people how to make better use of leisure time.

Some people who deeply feel the school's commitment to developing the potential of all children insist that the instructional program be broadened and adapted to the unique interests and abilities of gifted children, of slow learners, and of the great group of children commonly identified as "normal" or "average."

Others insist that the schools give more attention to adult education, to the conservation of natural resources, to education for the culturally disadvantaged, and to safety education.

Sometimes administrators become annoyed with these insistent and sometimes conflicting demands that converge on the superintendent's office and the school board meeting from every direction. Yet when they view them in perspective and assess them for their value, they cannot but see that herein lies the dynamics of educational improvement. Most people who advance these and other points of view and are ready to defend them with vigor are honest and sincere. These expressions of interest and concern are but the efforts of a nation of free people during a period of stress and strain to redefine their educational goals.

The infinite human variety in 50 million children and youth between the ages of 5 and 17 is too great for even the most capable demographers and social psychologists to comprehend and understand. Their family and community backgrounds, their unique interests and abilities, their physical and emotional characteristics are widely different. There is no common mold in which they can all be comfortably and conveniently placed. They live in lumber camps, in mining towns, in rural hamlets and villages, in sturdy homes on rich farmlands, in the flimsy dwellings of sharecroppers and migrant agricultural workers, in crowded quarters in the tenement districts of large cities, in stately homes along the avenue, and in the brand-new houses in the suburbs. Their names—Flanagan, O'Malley, Caballero, Wong, Yamasaki, Van Riper, MacGruder, Cohen, Gonzales, Jorgensen, Luigi, and Kazantzakis—suggest cultural streams that flow from many nations.

Some are academically gifted, while others have difficulty in mastering the basic skills of reading and writing; some have special aptitudes for music and the fine arts, while others are mechanically inclined; some are eagerly looking forward to continuing their education in a prestige college, while others are hoping for the day to come when they will no longer have to go to school. Most of them are ruddy and rugged, filled with youthful health and vigor, but some who are less fortunate carry physical, emotional, or mental handicaps.

A generation of youth is more than an incomprehensible statistic to be reasoned about, planned for, and treated as a huge impersonal entity. A generation of youth is the rosy-cheeked girl next door, the dashing halfback on the high school team, the president of the senior class, the little crippled boy who lives down the alley, and the habitual truant from the broken home who has had his first brush with the law. To think of a commitment to a generation of youth is to think of a commitment to each and every one of them.

To serve this generation of youth, to make every youngster know that he is really important and has a job to do, to make reason supreme and dominant over coercive force in every walk of life, and to develop in everyone whom the school reaches and serves the understanding and the power needed to keep the economy productive and to keep democracy working in the years ahead as well or better than it has worked in the past, it is imperative ⟶

TO MAKE URBAN LIFE REWARDING AND SATISFYING

Urbanization is one of the most pronounced phenomena of the times. People in great numbers are coming to large cities seeking better jobs, better education for their children, and a better way of life. They come on the crest of a rising wave of human aspirations. If these aspirations are to be realized—

All schools must have the best available instructional materials and equipment.

School plants must be designed and equipped to give pupils and teachers full opportunity for efficient and effective work.

Overcrowded classrooms and teacher shortages must be eliminated.

The instructional program must be extended downward to include kindergarten and prekindergarten-age children.

The educational program must be vitally related to the life of the community.

Inservice education programs for teachers must be greatly expanded.

Financial support must be greatly increased to provide the special services and the additional facilities necessary to meet the educational needs of great groups of children who have recently migrated to the cities.

•

TO PREPARE PEOPLE FOR THE WORLD OF WORK

Appropriate education stands squarely between the individual and the job he expects to get. At a time when the gross national product is at an all-time high and when demands for skilled workmen are increasing in many fields, thousands of young people ready to enter the labor market cannot find jobs because they lack the necessary qualifications. If this educational deficit is to be erased—

> Every child, youth, and adult must have as much education and as broad an education as his capacity will permit.
>
> High priority must be given to developing the knowledge essential for supporting economic enterprise and meeting manpower needs.
>
> Opportunities for technical and vocational training must be greatly extended and updated.
>
> Appropriate training in simple occupations must be provided for less-gifted students.
>
> The schools must take leadership in maintaining training and retraining programs for adults.
>
> Programs of vocational guidance must be extended and improved.

•

TO DISCOVER AND NURTURE CREATIVE TALENT

Individually and collectively the people of this country are looking to the schools for a great contribution toward developing the reservoir of creative power needed to meet and deal with challenges arising on the forefront of cultural change. To develop this potential—

> Every useful talent must be discovered and nurtured.
>
> Schools must lay the groundwork, kindle the curiosity, provide the skills, and create the incentives that motivate continued learning year after year.
>
> Pupil-teacher ratios must be maintained which permit teachers to meet the unique needs of every child.
>
> Every capable student must continue his formal education beyond the twelfth grade in an appropriate institution.
>
> Instruction in science, mathematics, and languages must begin in the elementary school and be continued and extended to the fullest degree student capacities will permit.
>
> Greater emphasis must be given to the humanities and the arts in the instructional program as a way to further develop the creative capacities of all students.

•

TO STRENGTHEN THE MORAL FABRIC OF SOCIETY

The basic values which undergird the American way of life and which have guided the actions of people for centuries are being put to a severe test in an era of rapid technological change, social readjustment, and population expansion. The results of this test are most visible where they apply to children and youth. If the schools are to be successful in helping young people develop values that will give them a sense of direction—

The dignity of each individual must be recognized and enhanced through the instructional program and the organization and operation of the school.

High priority in the instructional program must be given to the development of moral, spiritual, and ethical values.

Every child must be led to fully understand that freedom and responsibility go hand in hand.

All pupils must acquire a sense of values that will enable them to make intelligent decisions between right and wrong.

Commitment to common purposes above and beyond immediate selfish interests must be developed.

The true meaning of fair play, personal honor, and social justice must be exemplified in every facet of the school's operation.

•

TO DEAL CONSTRUCTIVELY WITH PSYCHOLOGICAL TENSIONS

Psychological tensions have been accentuated by, if they are not an actual outgrowth of, cultural change—change that has placed children and youth in new and vastly different situations. In unfortunate circumstances, these tensions have exploded into violent action; in less visible but equally important instances, they have impaired learning and blemished personalities. If the school is to help young people develop behavior patterns that will enable them to live without undue stress or conflict—

Children and youth must learn to meet and cope with social change.

A firm working alliance between the school and the home must be established.

Counseling and other supporting educational services must be provided to meet the needs of each student.

Every school must institute a continuing program of health education, multidisciplinary in nature and reaching pupils at every grade level, to develop the highest level of health attainable.

The school plant must provide an environment for pupils and teachers that is healthful, convenient, comfortable, and inspiring.

•

TO KEEP DEMOCRACY WORKING

The basic purpose of the school is to develop in all people the skills, understandings, beliefs, and commitments necessary for government of and by the people. This is in essence the responsibility for teaching citizenship—but teaching citizenship under a set of circumstances perhaps more trying than in former years. These circumstances are characterized by urbanization, powerful pressure groups, controversies over civil rights, and increasing interdependence between different parts of the country. To prepare a generation of young people for effective citizenship in these circumstances—

Every child must have proficiency in reading, writing, and the use of numbers.

Everyone must be led to recognize his privileges and to accept his responsibilities as an American citizen.

The schools must aid in developing the understandings, the skills, and the points of view essential for resolving broad cultural problems through reason and considered judgment.

The schools must not be dominated or unduly influenced by special interest groups and the changing tides of political pressures.

All forms of discrimination and racial and group prejudices must be eliminated from the schools.

Everyone must have an understanding of the basic principles of democracy and a commitment to uphold and to support them.

•

TO MAKE INTELLIGENT USE OF NATURAL RESOURCES

In keeping with the basic tenets of democracy, the control and use of natural resources have been entrusted to all the people. The question that now confronts everybody, and the schools in particular, is whether control of natural resources can continue to be left with the people or whether, because of dramatic increases in their use and misuse, regulatory measures will have to be imposed. The answer to this important question will depend in large measure upon whether—

All people—young children, adolescents, and adults—know and believe that natural resources are not inexhaustible.

Conservation is viewed as intelligent planning for efficient use, and not merely as saving.

Conservation is regarded as a problem based upon scientific principles firmly established in the laws of nature.

Extravagant use and waste leading to depletion of natural resources is eliminated.

Understandings and skills needed to deal with problems relative to the use of natural resources through community action and the processes of government are developed.

Students are involved in activities that will lead them to develop a sense of order among all things and to form concepts relative to the use of natural resources.

•

TO MAKE THE BEST USE OF LEISURE TIME

Leisure time was once a luxury for the few. Now it has become a privilege for the many. With each passing decade the amount of leisure time increases through shorter work weeks, unemployment, a longer life-span, laborsaving devices, and customs and legislative action that cause many people to retire while their minds are still active and their bodies still vigorous. If this leisure time is to be used for cultural betterment—

The schools must develop creative and imaginative programs to change the boredom of idle hours into fruitful and satisfying experiences.

Public libraries must cooperate with the schools in providing books and encouraging reading.

The schools must remain open until the late hours of the evening and throughout the summer months.

Creative writing, drama, art, music, and modern dance must be emphasized throughout the elementary and secondary grades.

Children must be taught how to relax in the out-of-doors and to appreciate and enjoy the beauty and wonders of nature.

Community choruses, orchestras, and little theater groups must be encouraged and supported.

Young people must be given opportunities to develop the leadership abilities and sense the satisfactions that come from participation in community service programs.

•

TO WORK WITH OTHER PEOPLES OF THE WORLD FOR HUMAN BETTERMENT

Through historical circumstances, a world leadership role has been thrust upon the United States. The hopes of people in other lands are kindled by the ideals and concepts that undergird the American way of life. Because of its strong commitments to maintaining peace; safeguarding the rights of freedom-loving people; and reducing poverty, ignorance, famine, and disease, it becomes increasingly important that the people of this country become familiar with the cultures of other lands and learn how to work in a fruitful manner with people whose customs, values, and traditions differ from their own. To meet this responsibility—

Every American must be led to support his country in its efforts to achieve its supreme goal of peace with freedom.

Students must become sensitive to the problems and circumstances prevailing in other nations and know the historical backgrounds of the people, their religious beliefs, their forms of government, and the problems they face.

Ways must be found to teach children how to respect deep-seated cultural values of other people without losing or diminishing in any degree their confidence, respect, and commitments to the ideals, values, and customs of their own country.

Instruction in foreign languages must be strengthened and extended.

•

The magnitude of these imperatives, which do not and are not intended to cover the entire program of public education, clearly shows that hopes for a quick and easy way to develop good schools are futile. There is no easy way to solve the school's problems—no easy way to provide for the individual differences of students, no easy way to motivate pupils to put forth greater effort, no easy way to bring about necessary improvements in the instructional program.

The institution of public education has not been created by following an easy course. It has not been built by clumsy artisans, nor has it reached the eminent place it now holds in this country and throughout the world through haphazard handling, incidental treatment, or "surefire" remedies. The vitality of the institution of public education and the force for human betterment that it exercises have emerged from experiences of people throughout the length and breadth of this country, laymen as well as professional educators, reaching upward for something better than they now have. The cherished qualities of the institution of public education have been built into it by the painstaking care and skillful molding of people who believe deeply in the importance of education, by people who understand the basic principles of how learning takes place and children mature, and by people with a sense of responsibility for the institution of public education which Horace Mann long ago asserted was the greatest creation of mankind.

INDEX OF NAMES

SUBJECT INDEX

F

G

H

I

J

K

L

M

U

V

W

Y